P9-CEY-355

THE FENG SHUI HANDBOOK

The author at the Lung Shan Temple in Taipei

THE FENG SHUI HANDBOOK

A Practical Guide to Chinese Geomancy and Environmental Harmony

DEREK WALTERS

Thorsons
An Imprint of HarperCollins*Publishers*

Thorsons
An Imprint of HarperCollins*Publishers*
77–85 Fulham Palace Road,
Hammersmith, London W6 8JB
1160 Battery Street,
San Francisco, California 94111–1213

Published by The Aquarian Press 1991
Published by Thorsons 1995
11 13 15 14 12

© Derek Walters 1991

Derek Walters asserts the moral right to
be identified as the author of this work

A catalogue record for this book
is available from the British Library

ISBN 0 85030 959 X

Typeset by MJL Limited,
Hitchin, Hertfordshire
Printed in Great Britain by
Woolnough Bookbinding Limited,
Irthlingborough, Northamptonshire

All rights reserved. No part of this publication may be
reproduced, stored in a retrieval system, or transmitted,
in any form or by any means, electronic, mechanical,
photocopying, recording or otherwise, without the prior
permission of the publishers.

Contents

Important Note

Throughout this book all maps and diagrams are shown according to the western convention, with North at the top, unless otherwise indicated. (Formerly, the Chinese convention, still retained in the practice of Feng Shui, was to show South at the top of maps, while Chinese compasses were South-pointing.)

Introduction

There is no single meaning of the expression 'Feng Shui'. In some contexts it can be translated as 'environment'. More usually, it refers to the 'feel' of a place, which some western people claim to be the result of its particular vibrations. The Chinese might even use the expression in a more limited sense, to mean simply a run of good or bad luck. Literally, the two characters for 'Feng' and 'Shui' signify 'wind and water'; this may convey little meaning in itself, but it does hint at the origins of the art of Feng Shui. Perhaps the best way to explain Feng Shui is to think of it as the terrestrial equivalent of astrology—as such, a subject that has no parallel in western experience. Thus while astrology, familiar to both Chinese and western cultures, seeks to find what Fate holds in store from signs in the skies above us, Feng Shui, its earth-bound counterpart, takes its omens from the earth below. More specifically, in astrology note is taken of the movement and appearance of celestial bodies; in Feng Shui observations are made of the hills and streams that surround a particular spot.

There is, however, one significant difference. The planets cannot be stopped in their courses, but the face of a landscape can be changed—for good or ill. The Chinese have long been believers that any interference with the terrain—whether by cutting canals, excavating tunnels, laying railway lines, or erecting huge buildings that distort the original forms of the skyline— can bring about unforeseen calamities. To take just one catastrophic example: in the USSR, diverting the rivers that fed the Aral Sea, in order to irrigate the arid plains of southern Central Asia, resulted in the virtual disappearance of the Aral Sea itself, not only reducing thousands of square miles of once beautiful countryside to an arid waste, but also causing the formation of terrible dehydrating salt storms that travelled hundreds of miles beyond the parched beds of the dried-up sea, resulting in the destruction of life on a unimagined scale.

The hazards of environmental change are rarely on such an awesome scale. Yet even the ancients knew that building high towers resulted in the creation of gusting winds of unforeseen force, or that the digging of wells could cause streams to dry up. Thus the Chinese observed how the wayward influences of 'winds and waters' could be affected by alterations to the shape of the earth's existing contours. And if such minor changes to the earth's constitution were able to influence such powerful agencies as the winds and waters, what effect might they therefore not have on such a fragile matter as the state of human affairs?

The principles of Feng Shui are based on precepts laid down thousands of years ago in the Chinese classics, particularly the *Li Shu*, or *Book of Rites*, a sacred book that enshrines the basic tenets of Chinese religious belief. It is concerned with order, the harmony of heaven and earth, and with the ways in which humanity can best keep the balance of nature intact.

Today, Feng Shui is a complex blend of common-sense maxims,

The spectacular scenery of southern China, where Yang Yun-sung formulated the principles of the Form School of Feng Shui

logical reasoning, and oral traditions, some of which are frankly no more substantial than peasant superstitions, superimposed on a highly sophisticated discipline based on the points of the compass, and with its own rich symbolism.

In the ninth century AD, two great scholars, working from two entirely different viewpoints, decided to commit their opinions to paper. Thus it was that in the wonderful surroundings of Kuei-lin, among its bizarrely sculpted hills and mountains, the sage Yang Yun-sung compiled the first manual of Feng Shui, systematically describing the characteristics of scenic formations. This book was to become the standard text on the Form School of Feng Shui. Then, about a century later, scholars living in the flat plains of the north composed their own answer to the problems of analysing the Feng Shui of mountainless regions, compiling a guide to another system of Feng Shui founded on the symbolism of the points of the compass. This 'Compass School', or Fukien method, for practical reasons, proved to be immensely influential. Today, Feng Shui experts combine the two systems, looking first at the undulations of the surrounding countryside, and then consulting the compass to note the alignments of the surrounding mountains and rivers with the spot under consideration.

In addition to these two major schools of thought is what might be called the 'Third' school of Feng Shui—a motley collection of odd maxims and folklore drawn partly from common-sense observation, and partly from a vivid imagination. This book is principally concerned with the two main schools of thought—the Form School and the Compass School—which have not only been sanctified by time, but have a scientific foundation for their principles. A few remarks on the 'Third' method of Feng Shui have been added, in view of their universal acceptance.

This book begins by showing the reader how to examine the surrounding landscape, whether a country panorama or an urban skyline, and identify its potential Feng Shui qualities. The technical and complex details of the Compass School are introduced one by one, and readers are constantly encouraged to test their understanding of the text by completing simple exercises on each new facet of information.

Perhaps the most intriguing part of this book is the section showing how everybody can match their personal characteristics to their surroundings, whether at home or at work, thus ensuring greater environmental harmony and leading to enhanced inner peace, which itself leads to happiness, personal success, and fortune.

This cannot be a complete guide to the enormous subject of Feng Shui, but it is rather more than just an introduction. There are many areas that have been deliberately left untouched—particularly the subject of 'Yin Chai' Feng Shui, or the orientation of grave sites. Nor has the reader been expected to acquire a knowledge of Chinese characters, essential to a full understanding of the Chinese *Lo P'an* (described in Chapter 8). Nevertheless, it is fair to say that those readers who complete and understand this book thoroughly will not just have been introduced to the basic principles of Feng Shui; they will have become as conversant with its mysteries as many practising geomancers in the Far East.

1

The Nature of Feng Shui

This opening chapter begins by inviting you to look at the scenic features of your neighbourhood, or the surrounding area of your place of work, by taking note of all the shapes and features that make up the skyline and panorama around you.

This may seem irrelevant to anyone who had imagined that Feng Shui was all about house or shop interiors. When all they want to know is which direction their bed should face, or whether the back room should be the kitchen or the conservatory, the emphasis on certain details at the outset might appear over-technical.

There is a popular impression that Feng Shui is little more than a kind of mystic interior design, but the subject is actually far more profound. In order to give the answers to such apparently simple matters as those above, many varied factors have to be taken into account, among them being the surrounding features, the direction the house faces, and even—not least important—how the residents are considered to interact with the house itself. Indeed, the formidable technicalities of Feng Shui are the very reason why most Chinese people prefer to call in an expert, who is aware of details that might otherwise be forgotten or overlooked, rather than try to tackle the job themselves.

When called upon to visit a site for professional advice, the Feng Shui practitioner first takes note of the surrounding area, examining certain aspects of the scenery and neighbouring buildings, then takes the next crucial step: making a careful note of the alignment of the site in relation to the directions of the compass. For this reason, this book begins, logically, by looking at the features of the surrounding skyline that affect, for good or bad, the Feng Shui at a particular spot.

The earliest writers on Feng Shui stated that the very best sites were those which were on the south-facing side of a hill, with a rivulet running at one side of the house, the stream then turning in front of the site to disappear underground. This specification, of course, can be attributed to plain common sense. The south-facing side of a hill not only receives the maximum benefit of the sun, but, with the hill behind, both crops and buildings are protected from the north winds. Being on a slope, neither at the foot of the hill nor the top, the site affords natural protection against marauders, who would first have to climb the hill before they could gain any downward advantage. Conversely, if the house was at the foot of the hill, there would be a danger of flooding. The provision of water (seldom found at the top of a hill) is all-important, not only to sustain life, but also for cleansing purposes. For this reason it is preferably for soiled water to disappear out of sight. Today, Feng Shui enshrines these principles in a canon of flexible theories, all derived from ancient maxims on what is essentially the subject of land surveying.

Definitions

When we talk about the Feng Shui of a particular place, are we referring to the Feng Shui of the area itself, or one particular spot, or a building yet to be erected, or the rooms within a building which already exists, or to one of many other possible situations?

In this book, precise definitions have been given to a few words which, in everyday language, could be used in a wider sense. There is no need to memorize these definitions: they are only intended for clarity.

Site

The term SITE is used to mean the particular defined place which is being investigated. It may be a plot of ground on which it is proposed to build, or a building that is already in existence.

Location

The LOCATION surrounds the SITE. The LOCATION is usually limited by the extent of the surroundings that are visible from the SITE.

Environment

ENVIRONMENT refers to the qualities, good or bad, of the LOCA-
TION. The qualities are determined by the ENVIRONMENTAL FEA-
TURES, which may be natural or man-made features of the
ENVIRONMENT discernible at the SITE.

Orientation

ORIENTATION refers to the direction faced by the SITE. It is found
by reference to a magnetic compass. Chinese Feng Shui experts
use a special kind of compass, which will be described later in
this book, but for the moment, any ordinary magnetic compass
will serve the purpose.

We can now look at some of these definitions a little more closely,
to see what they imply.

The Site

The following are all examples of SITES:

> Building Plot No. 275
> White Barn Field, Sheepfold Farm
> Silbury Hill
> 26, Smith Road
> Flat 27b, William and Mary Mansions
> Woolley's Dry Goods Store
> The Adelphi Theatre
> Buckingham Palace

In addition, since the Chinese also pay great attention to the
desirability of good Feng Shui in searching for a burial place for
their deceased relatives, there would also be other examples of
'burial' sites, which the Chinese refer to as 'Yin' houses, meaning, elliptically, dwellings for the dead.

The Location

The LOCATION may be in a sparsely populated area, where the
limits of visibility are determined by the panorama and may be
very extensive, or conversely, in a highly built-up area where the
vista is limited by the walls of immediately adjacent buildings.

The Environment

The purpose of the study of Feng Shui is to assess the ENVIRON-
MENTAL QUALITIES of a location, and determine whether these
are beneficial or adverse, and to suggest ways in which the adverse
qualities may be avoided and the beneficial ones harnessed to
make the maximum use of their effectiveness.

Environmental Features

ENVIRONMENTAL FEATURES may be natural, or man-made. It can
be assumed that natural features are superior to man-made ones.
Examples of natural features are:

> Mountains, hills, and prominences
> Unusually formed rock shapes
> Unusual silhouettes of hills on the skyline
> Large isolated trees, particularly conifers
> Groups of trees
> Lakes, ponds, and seashore
> Rivers and streams
> Waterfalls
> Veins in rocks
> Valleys and gulleys
> Notches in the skyline

Examples of man-made features that affect the Feng Shui are:

> Fields
> Hedges
> Canals, sluices, conduits
> Ponds, reservoirs
> Fountains
> Roads
> Bridges
> Railways
> Telegraph wires
> Quarries
> Tunnels
> Mines
> Cuttings

The above list of features can be considered, broadly, as environmental features in the rural sense. Urban features, though smaller in scale, are more complex. They can be divided, roughly, into groups:

Utilities:
>   Telegraph poles
>   Telephone wires
>   Lamp posts
>   Drains, culverts
>   Gas pipes, conduits

Residential:
>   Houses
>   Blocks of flats
>   Terraces
>   Mansions
>   Cottages

and their adjuncts:
>   Roads
>   Driveways
>   Gardens
>   Ponds

Memorial and monumental:
>   Obelisks
>   Ceremonial gates
>   Triumphal arches
>   Commemorative pillars
>   Open squares
>   Market-places
>   Schools, churches, hospitals, public buildings
>   Monuments and follies
>   Public buildings
>   Places of entertainment

Military:
>   Castles
>   Fortifications
>   Battlements
>   Ancient walls
>   Man-made hills

Industrial:

> Chimneys
> Pylons
> Gas-holders
> Storage tanks
> Cooling towers

In a heavily built-up area even more man-made features impinge on the Feng Shui of a location:

> Proximity of other buildings
> Proximity of walls and windows
> Shapes of roofs against the skyline
> Blank walls
> Alley ways
> Walls of buildings forming angles
> Unusual ornamentations of roofs
> Direction of roads and driveways
> Stairways
> Utility pipes: drains; water; gas

Later we shall look at the importance and effect of such features. In the meantime, however, the reader is asked to carry out the following exercise.

Exercise

Go to the nearest window, and using the above list as a guide note as many environmental features as possible. Then, move to a window that faces another direction and repeat the exercise. If in both cases you have been unlucky, and chanced upon a window that faces a blank wall, find a suitable view that provides as many features as possible. Find at least twenty features.

The Basic Principles of Feng Shui

Once the reader is familiar with those features of the environment that are likely to affect the Feng Shui of a site, the question remains whether features which are beneficial from one site may be harmful to another. For this reason, the reader is asked to remember the following principles, which may not be immediately self-evident. The accompanying diagrams will no doubt be clearer than the text, and should therefore be scrutinized carefully.

Axiom 1

Although the environmental features may be the same for neighbouring sites within any given location, the qualities of those features will vary according to the actual position of each site within that location.

Axiom 1: The qualities of a feature vary according to the position of the sites

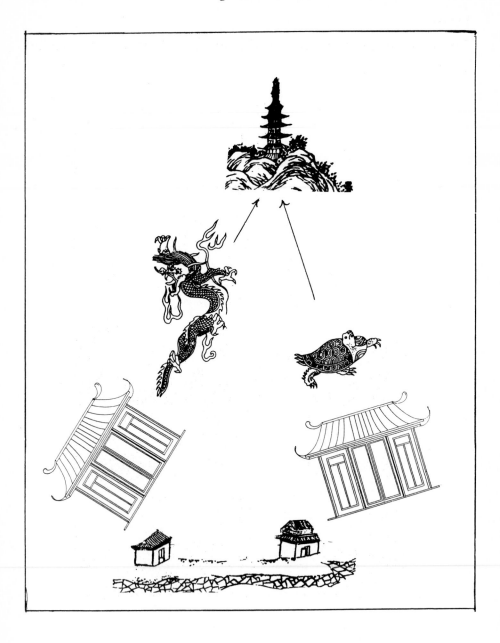

Analysis of Axiom 1: The pagoda is situated at the Dragon side
of the house on the left but at the Tortoise side of the house
on the right

Axiom 2

The environmental features for a site vary according to the site's orientation.

Axiom 2: The Dragon mountain lies in the same direction for all the houses in this village, although each house's orientation is different

The Feng Shui Handbook

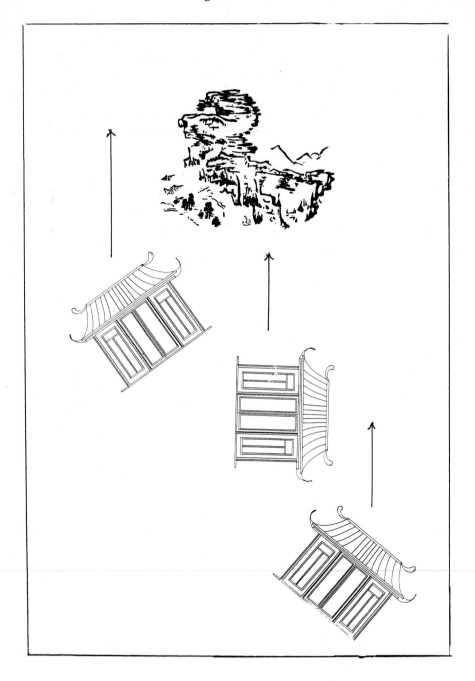

Analysis of Axiom 2: The three houses are all to the same side of
the mountain, but each is orientated differently

Special Terms used in Feng Shui

Feng Shui uses special terms taken from Chinese astronomy (Bird, Tortoise, Dragon and Tiger) to represent the four directions—front, back, right, and left respectively. In ordinary terms, the four 'celestial' animals are associated with the four compass points and the four seasons as follows:

Dragon	Spring	East
Bird	Summer	South
Tiger	Autumn	West
Tortoise	Winter	North

For comparison, here is a reminder of the Feng Shui use of the terms:

Dragon	right
Bird	front
Tiger	left
Tortoise	back

When the front of a site faces the South, then the four Feng Shui terms correspond with the four compass directions. But for the

The East-facing house   The South-facing house

The West-facing house   The North-facing house

reasons that will become clear later, the two sets of terms are not interchangeable. To appreciate the difference between the Feng Shui terms and the conventional use of the points of the compass, consider the ways that Feng Shui applies the terms to the four sides of a building. For a building or apartment, the BIRD side is the one that has the entrance; the TORTOISE is the opposite side, which should be the back of the building. Then, if one stands in the building and looks at the front, or bird side, the DRAGON side will be on one's left, and the TIGER on one's right.

In a house of conventional design, if the entrance faces south, and the back door faces north, the Four Directions—North, East, South, and West—will be represented by the Tortoise, Dragon, Bird, and Tiger respectively.

Facing Walls

Internal and external walls are called by the direction they face. In the diagram at right, the entrance is represented by the Bird, as is also the interior facing wall, B. But the exterior wall, A, belongs to the Tortoise. Similarly, external wall F and internal wall D face the Dragon, while external wall C and internal wall E face the Tiger. Thus, while an architect or a builder may refer, for example, to walls E and F as the east wall, in Feng Shui terms, E is Tiger-facing, and F Dragon-facing.

A

B

C   D   E   F

When the Feng Shui of a locality is being assessed, the four animal names may be applied to the four points of the compass. As each animal has its own appropriate colour, the four directions can be said to be:

North	Black Tortoise
East	Green Dragon
South	Red Bird
West	White Tiger

It is interesting to note that many modern Chinese Feng Shui practitioners, particularly in Hong Kong and South China, have dropped the term 'Tortoise' and use instead the word 'Warrior'. Both terms, Warrior and Tortoise, have been in use since the first century at least, and it is not clear when, or why, the Warrior became an alternative to the Tortoise. The Tortoise, however, in Taoism and Bon Buddhism, is the symbol of the universe, and is probably the more authentic term.

Feng Shui theory declares that the very best possible site for a building is one where the four symbols—Dragon, Bird, Tiger, and Tortoise—are readily distinguishable in the shapes of the surrounding scenery. If all four symbols are not apparent, it is regarded as fortunate if just three of them can be discerned; if not three, then the Dragon on its own; and if not the Dragon, then merely the Tiger will serve to establish the presence of the four emblems. Above all, for good Feng Shui, the symbol of the Dragon should be visible, and the geomancer's first priority, in examining the site, is to see what distant hill or promontory can be said to fulfil the role of the Dragon.

The Dragon and the Tiger always co-exist and are inseparable, just as a magnet must have a south and a north pole. If there is a Dragon, there will be a spot called the Tiger, even though it may not be visible. Similarly, if the landscape is very plain, and it is not possible to see the Dragon, but there is a hill in the west which serves as the Tiger, then by default the Dragon must also be present, even if not evident.

The Ideal Setting

The ideal setting is one in which there are two hills, one to the east of the location, the other to the west. The Dragon always

Dragon and Tiger in an embrace

being superior to the Tiger, the eastern hill, representing the Dragon, will be slightly higher, more prominent, and more rugged than the western hill. When one hill continues behind the other, this is considered to be even more beneficial and is said to represent the Dragon and Tiger in an embrace.

The North can be represented by more distant and higher mountains, although suitably positioned conifers are also regarded as symbolic of the Black Tortoise. The southern aspect should be open, indeed it is even better if there is a depression on the southern aspect. Chinese houses and temples built according to Feng Shui criteria will have a sunken courtyard or pool in front of the building to emphasize this principle. Farther in the distance, however, it should ideally be possible to identify a rock, or some other feature which represents the Feng Shui Red Bird. It will not, notice, be a dominant object, such as a tree or pole, which might overshadow the building, as this would be a sign of bad Feng Shui, as will be seen later.

The function of a hill or other feature of the skyline as a Dragon or Tiger only holds for its observation from a particular location. Thus, any promontory is likely to be both a Dragon and a Tiger, being a Dragon when seen from a point to the west of it, but a Tiger when seen from a vantage point on its eastern side. Whether it is effective as a Dragon or Tiger will depend on the hill which forms its partner.

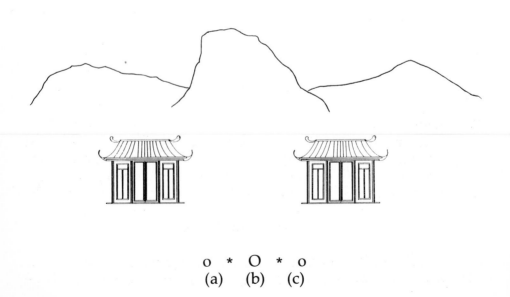

o * O * o
(a)   (b)   (c)

In the first diagram, (a) and (c) are small hills, (b) a much larger hill. From a site between (a) and (b), (a) will be seen as the Tiger, and (b) as the Dragon; the latter being dominant, the Dragon will be more powerful than the Tiger, which is good Feng Shui. But from a vantage point between the hills (b) and (c), the larger hill, (b) will be regarded as the Tiger, which is not as satisfactory.

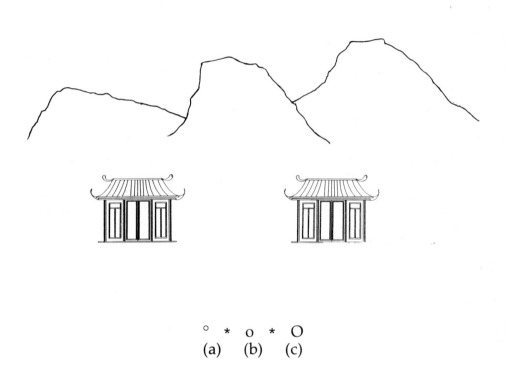

∘   *   o   *   O

(a)   (b)   (c)

In the second diagram, (c) is the largest of the three hills. Thus, from the first site, the Dragon and the Tiger will be in their most appropriate places. From the second site, however, the vantage point regards hill (b) as the Tiger, but the third hill (c), dominating (b), will be the Dragon, which is much more satisfactory.

Dragon qualities

Chinese Feng Shui practitioners claim that the more a hill or sky-line resembles an actual Dragon, the greater are the beneficial

The Confucian Temple at Kaohsiung. Notice the 'Dragon' hill in the background, and the wide courtyard, or Ming T'ang, in front of the Temple

influences of the Feng Shui. Thus, the expert geomancer looks not merely for a hill on the eastern side of the location, but makes every effort to discern the Dragon's limbs and features in the physical terrain. A raised head, for example, is extremely fortunate. Groves of trees might be said to be its eyebrows, and gulleys its veins. But most fortunate of all is the existence of a pool or stream under the dragon's mouth, as this is said to represent the classic image of the 'Dragon salivating pearls'—a sure sign that whoever builds in such a favourable spot will acquire riches and wealth.

It is regarded as being very hazardous to build, construct, or in any way cut across features that the geomancer declares to be parts of a Dragon's body. Trees that outline its form are 'Feng Shui' trees and must not be cut down. The worst calamities, however, befall those who slice across the Dragon's veins, for this kills the Dragon and bring calamities upon the household of whoever has acted so intrepidly. The basis for this firmly established belief can be traced back to the fact that the veins of the Dragon are usually formed over the centuries by being the channels for excess water at times of great flooding. Though they may become streams only once every score or so, they have been carved over the ages and are silent indicators of where future flooding may occur. Houses, fields, or roads constructed in these places, which can be deceptively verdant and scenic, have their foundations laid as precariously as on shifting sands. In a similar way, many of the other apparently groundless maxims of Feng Shui are actually based on sound commonsense.

Review

The Four Directions, (forwards, backwards, left, and right) are symbolized by four emblems:

Tortoise

Tiger   Dragon

Bird

* The four emblems may equate to the four points of the compass, but only when orientation of a building is south facing.

* The Dragon-direction is the most important of the Four Directions.

Feng Shui Pagodas representing the geomantic Dragon and Tiger, near Kaohsiung

* The Dragon and Tiger are mutually existent; if there is a Dragon there must be a Tiger, even if not apparent, and vice versa.

* If the Dragon and the Tiger are discernible, it is best for the Dragon to dominate the Tiger.

* It is favourable when the Dragon or Tiger wraps round the other: this is said to be the 'Dragon and Tiger' in an embrace.

* It is considered to be very favourable when the features of the Dragon are discernible in the scenery.

* It is considered unfavourable to carry out any works that destroy the discernible features of the Dragon.

Exercise

* Visit various localities, noting hills that might be regarded as Dragon or Tiger hills.
* Decide which would be the most favourable place to build within the area.

2

The Site

Although we have scrutinized the skyline and noted all the possible shapes and features that are likely to affect the Feng Shui of the location, we have yet to discover whether these features are favourable or otherwise—something that can only be assessed once some knowledge of the basic principles of Feng Shui has been attained. For the time being, then, our checklists of environmental features, our notes on the positions of the Dragon and the Tiger, and our sketch plans, if we have made any, can be left to one side while we take a look at the site itself, considering one of the basic principles of Feng Shui, namely, the topic of *ch'i*, the good influences, and *sha*, the bad ones.

Ch'i

The word *ch'i* is a much used, even overworked, term in the Chinese sciences. Among its variety of meanings are 'breath', 'air', 'fortnight', and, in modern chemistry, 'gas', while it has an even wider usage in such subjects as acupuncture. In Feng Shui, however, the term is generally understood to mean favourable currents, particularly the beneficial influences that might be brought to a site by a well-positioned Dragon hill, but equally may apply to healthy currents of air flowing through a room.

As the reader will have gathered, the presence of a well-sited and well-defined Dragon hill generates an abundance of positive *ch'i*, which not only produces a healthy environment and prolongs the expectation of life but, by promoting a harmonious and happy atmosphere within the home or a workplace, is also able to bring prosperity in a material sense as well.

Ch'i should be encouraged to enter the site and meander

through it before leaving at the opposite side. In rooms that need a lively environment, such as a living-room or workroom, *ch'i* can be encouraged to energize the area by being reflected back and forth by carefully positioned mirrors. Conversely, in rooms that are meant to be restful, such as bedrooms or lounges, *ch'i* should be funnelled gently round the room. For this reason, it is not a good idea for bedrooms to have mirrors, as these excite the *ch'i*, making the atmosphere stimulating rather than restful. On the other hand, in hotels that are favoured, let us say, by honeymooners, the provision of mirrors can be a welcome addition.

Obviously, if there is no exit for the *ch'i*, they will be unable to leave; the same door or window cannot admit *ch'i* and let them leave at the same time. For example, a room without windows and only one door lacks the means to let the *ch'i* circulate. Such rooms, in which the *ch'i* die and become stagnant, are really only suitable for storerooms and cupboards.

Sha

The converse of *ch'i* is *sha*, which are said to be the carriers of unfavourable currents that have an adverse effect on the family obliged to reside in that unfortunate spot. The function of the Feng Shui expert is to advise how the beneficial *ch'i* may be harnessed to permeate the home with its life-enhancing powers and how to deflect the unfavourable *sha* from exerting their influences.

It is generally accepted that beneficial *ch'i* waft slowly, in gentle undulating curves, while *sha* travel in harsh straight lines. For the moment, we shall look at the kinds of situations that are regarded as producing harmful *sha*.

(a) Geographical faults

Sha are produced by geographical faults and fissures in the earth. Feng Shui would declare that the city of San Francisco is situated in one of the worst locations possible, on account of the 'San Andreas' fault, which would be deemed to produce highly adverse *sha*. (Western geologists would come to the same conclusion, though for entirely different reasons.) Curiously enough, despite this, San Francisco not only continues to be a thriving

city, but it also has one of the largest Chinese communities outside China!

Natural gulleys that form straight lines directed at the site also
produce *sha*. These may at one time have been river-beds, though
now dried up; but they could be quiescent sources of danger in
a time of exceptional rainfall, as they would carry flood waters
directly to the site.

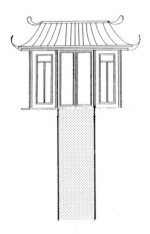

Sha produced by straight lines

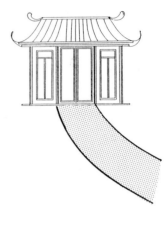

Ch'i flow in gentle curves

'Secret arrow' caused by angle
of the house

'Secret arrow' caused by bend
in road

(b) Buildings and roads

Corners of buildings that have the angle pointing at the site are deemed to be the source of a special kind of *sha* known as a 'secret arrow'. The angle is considered to be a bow, poised with its threatening arrow direct at the site. People living in such a spot are likely to suffer from continual illnesses, and the atmosphere is said to be debilitating.

The edges of buildings, almost always associated with roads, paths, passageways and alleyways leading towards the front door of the house, are considered to encourage *sha* to be directed at the house. Actually, in the case of roads leading up to a house, the inherent dangers from fast traffic may indeed be greater nowadays than they were in former times. Roads that lead up to a house and then turn at a sharp right angle are considered to be especially harmful, combining the ill-effects of both ordinary *sha* and the secret arrow.

Although the subject of tunnels and railway lines is actually something to be considered when looking at the location, rather than the site, nevertheless, when tunnels or railways approach the site with the same proximity that roads nearly always do they should be regarded as potential carriers of *sha*.

(c) Interior structures

A house that is divided by a central passageway, or one that has the back door opposite and visible from the front door, is not regarded as a favourable site. Although the central passageway acts as a carrier for baleful *sha*, it is the fact that it causes the rapid dispersion of favourable *ch'i* that is the main problem. The rational explanation is that a house built in this manner tends to become a house divided against itself; those members of the family living mainly on one side of the house subconsciously become a counter-party to those living on the other side of the divide. Another explanation is that a central passageway makes it easy for burglars and sneak thieves to assess the security of a household.

There are two other structural arrangements that are considered bad from a Feng Shui point of view. The first is the western 'sunshine' or 'through' lounge which has windows opposite each other. In such a room, there is no fixed point, no sense of repose. As a lounge, therefore, the design fails. Feng Shui explains the

Chinese houses avoid having the staircase facing the door

sense of unease by pointing out that helful *ch'i* pass right through the room, without having a chance to release their beneficial influences.

Most likely for the same reasons, Chinese people do not favour the western practice of having stairs directly opposite the front door. Chinese prefer to have the stairs away from the front door, perhaps on a side wall, and, if possible, turning at the half flight.

(d) Service cables

Telegraph wires and power cables are no less unsightly in the city than they are in the country, but from a Feng Shui viewpoint they are also regarded as modern-day conductors of unfavourable *sha*. If they must approach the building, it is better for them to do so at an oblique angle, almost parallel with the exterior wall.

(e) Columns, posts and poles

Associated with telegraph wires are the telegraph poles themselves. Neither these, nor lamp-posts, nor tall trees, should be positioned outside a front window. They represent the conifers of the north, and being on the 'Bird' side of the building, are therefore inappropriate to that place.

Sometimes builders go to extraordinary lengths to avoid straight
paths leading directly to a building

Another opinion is that such tall columns cast malignant *sha*
over the site by virtue of their unfavourable straight shadows. As
an interesting sidelight on this point, I was told by a Chinese Feng
Shui enthusiast that the dissolution of the British Empire was
foretold by the erection of a monumental column in front of Buck-
ingham Palace. Asked by a Chinese friend to comment on this
point, I remarked that the monument actually broke the unfavourable *sha* of the Mall (the ceremonial approach to the Palace) by
causing traffic to veer round the central island, whereas formerly the Mall approached the Palace directly, and then turned at
a right angle.

For the moment, there follows a summary of the principal sources of *ch'i* and *sha*. In a later section, we shall investigate ways of removing the unfavourable influences from the site.

Summary of Points Regarding Ch'i

A well-defined Dragon and Tiger produce good *ch'i*.
Ch'i move in gentle curved lines.
They should be encouraged to find a route which takes them round the site.
They cannot leave by the same way they entered.
Cupboards and enclosed spaces exhaust the benefits of *ch'i*.
Mirrors can be used to deflect the course of *ch'i*.

Summary of Potential Sha

Natural geographical faults.
Gulleys
Tunnels
Corners of buildings
Edges of buildings
Roads and pathways
Central passageways within a building
'Through' rooms with windows at each end
Staircases opposite doors
Telegraph wires
Telegraph poles, lamp-posts, tall trees.

玉川居士

龍團嘗罷清風生腋睡魔降

鳳餅煎來活火騰炻玄鶴避

3

The Five Elements

Central to Feng Shui theory is the principle of the Five Elements. Whenever a Feng Shui expert studies the hills or buildings that surround a site, or considers whether the prospective site matches the personality of the client, or even advises on the material and colour of the furnishings within a room, all the deliberations and counsel will be based on the interaction of the predominant element, whether Wood, Fire, Earth, Metal, or Water.

This order of the elements is the principal one, because in this order each element is seen to *generate* the next one.

Thus:

Wood	burns, creating
Fire	which leaves ash, or
Earth	from which is obtained
Metal	which can be melted to flow like
Water	which is needed to sustain growing
Wood	and so on.

Through the Five Element theory, the Chinese are able to classify all things into one of five categories. The expression 'Five Elements' has been adopted for convenience, since they apparently parallel the four Aristotelian elements—Air, Earth, Fire, and Water. Some writers prefer to call the five Chinese categories by other terms, such as the 'five agencies' but since the expression 'elements' has been in use for at least three hundred years there seems to be little point in changing it now. Nevertheless, the five Chinese elements and the four western elements have little in common other than the names of three of them. But there all similarity ceases. To begin with, the four western elements form complementary and contrasting pairs; whereas in the Chinese system, the very fact that there are five elements creates a continual imbalance, which is itself the essential kernel of the Chinese philosophy of continual change.

The Five Planets

The fact that there are five Chinese elements seems to be derived from the fact that ancient astronomers recognized five major planets; and indeed, the five inner planets are known as the Wood Planet (Jupiter); the Fire Planet (Mars); the Earth Planet (Saturn); the Metal Planet (Venus); and the Water Planet (Mercury). The names of the planets are given here out of interest only, and neither they nor the apparent confusion between Saturn and the Earth need concern us further.

The Five Elements and the Five Cardinal Points

The Five Elements symbolize the Five Cardinal Points, namely, the Four Directions—East, South, West, and North—together with the non-direction, Centre. Earlier, we saw that each of the Four Directions represented one of the seasons: East, the Spring; South, the Summer; West, Autumn; and North, Winter. Now by omitting (for the time being) the central Earth element, the Four Directions symbolize the four seasons, their colours, and four of the elements, thus:

East	Spring	Green	Wood
South	Summer	Red	Fire
Centre		Yellow	Earth
West	Autumn	White	Metal
North	Winter	Black	Water

These correlations are explained by the fact that in Spring, plant life (the Chinese word for 'Wood' is wide-reaching) begins to grow, showing green buds, while Spring is the dawn of the new year and the sun rises in the East. Similarly, red is the colour of Fire; the sun is at its hottest at midday, when it is in the South; Summer is the noon of the year. Yellow is the colour of the earth of central China. Autumn is the time of harvesting, and also when in ancient times, after the harvesting, it was customary to fight wars. For sickles in peacetime, or swords in times of war, Metal was needed, and white (silvery white) is the colour of polished iron. Winter is the midnight of the year, when all is black and the sunshine gives way to rains, hence Water is the element of Winter and the North.

Generative and Destructive Orders

The 'generative' order of the elements has already been given. This is the basic order of the Five Elements and should be remembered. It can be shown diagrammatically:

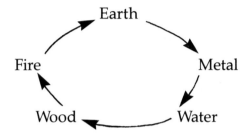

Generative Order of the Elements

Elements that are next to each other in this order help each other; thus Wood helps Fire, Water helps Wood, and so on. But there is another order of the elements, called the 'destructive' order. When two elements stand next to each other in this series, one destroys the other.

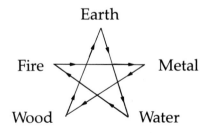

Destructive Order of the Elements

So Wood destroys Earth, Fire destroys Water, and so on. The sequence can be remembered by thinking:

Wood draws the goodness from Earth

Earth pollutes Water
Water quenches Fire
Fire melts Metal
Metal chops down Wood

On the other hand, observe that some elements act to the advantage of others in the reverse order; for example, Earth nourishes Wood; Water softens Earth (making clay pliable); and Fire boils Water.

When someone assesses the Feng Shui qualities of a site, it is important to see what are the predominant elements of the surroundings, and then decide what is likely to be the predominant element of the site. In this way it will be possible to ensure that the elemental qualities of the location and the site will be in harmony.

Firstly, then, let us look at the ways in which the elemental qualities are revealed.

Shape

Perhaps the most obvious way by which a location reveals its elemental qualities is in its *shape*. We see opposite the shapes associated with each of the elements.

Wood. Trees are tall and upright. The Wood element is suggested by columnar structures such as tall soaring hills (such as those found in parts of southern China), or in man-made structures such as pillars, minarets, factory chimneys, or tall narrow skyscraper buildings.

Fire. Points suggest flames. The Fire element is represented by the sharp peaks of mountains, and by the steeply-pointed roofs of certain eastern temples, the spires of churches, and similar sharply-roofed buildings.

Earth. The ground is generally flat; the Earth element is shown by long, flat hills, plateaux, table mountains, and flat-roofed buildings.

Metal. Bronze mirrors and coins are round; the Metal element is shown in gently-rounded summits of hills, and by buildings that have domed roofs.

Water. Water has no shape and every shape. The Water element is revealed in undulating and irregular hills, and by buildings that have bizarre or complex structures, although rounded rather than angular.

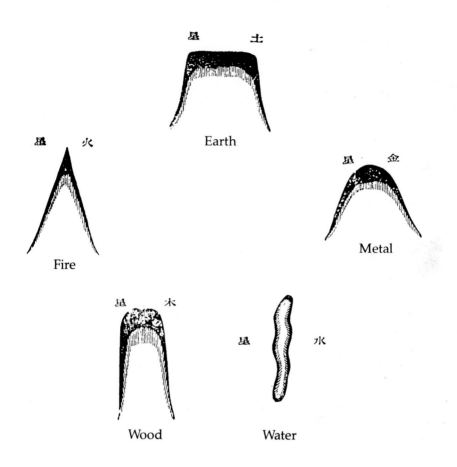

The Five Elemental Shapes

Exercises

1. Which elements are associated with:

(a) Spring   (b) Winter

(c) Green   (d) Yellow

(e) South   (f) East

(g) Tortoise   (h) Dragon

(i) Sunset   (j) Noon

2. What element
   produces:
(a) Earth   (b) Water
     destroys:
(c) Fire   (d) Metal
     is produced by:
(e) Wood   (f) Earth
     is destroyed by:
(g) Water   (h) Fire

Answers

1. (a) Wood (b) Water (c) Wood (d) Earth (e) Fire (f) Wood (g) Water
(h) Wood (i) Metal (j) Fire

2. (a) Fire (b) Metal (c) Water (d) Fire (e) Fire (f) Metal (g) Fire (h)
Metal

Element Shapes in Practice

We should now consider the Feng Shui situation that would be
the consequence of erecting a building of a particular shape, in
surroundings dominated by buildings, or hills, with well-defined
element features.

With the two sequences discussed above, we could imagine five
possible cases, when the element of the surrounding is the SAME
as the element of the contemplated structure, either precedes or
follows it in the GENERATIVE sequence, or further, precedes or
follows it in the DESTRUCTIVE sequence. To take an example; suppose the predominant element of the surroundings (the element
of the location) is the Earth element, revealed by squarish, flat-
topped buildings. It is proposed to erect another building within
this location, but its general shape has not yet been decided. The
proposed structure might have any of the five elemental shapes:
Wood (tall and slender); Fire (pointed); Earth (flat topped); Metal
(rounded); or Water (irregular).

These are the five situations:

1. *Location: Earth/Structure: Wood*
   Earth and Wood are in the destructive sequence, Wood benefit-

ing at the expense of Earth. This would be very fortunate for those working or living in the proposed building.

2. *Location: Earth/Structure: Fire*
Earth and Fire are in the generative sequence, Earth benefiting from Fire. The situation would not be harmful, but on the other hand not very rewarding. It would be an ideal situation, however, for a hospital, school, or library—buildings intended to be of benefit to the community.

3. *Location: Earth/Structure: Earth*
Earth and Earth are stable; the situation is neither beneficial nor harmful. In cases like this, the structure should have the same purpose as the buildings round it, such as a new residential block in a residential area, for example.

4. *Location: Earth/Structure: Metal*
Earth and Metal are in the generative sequence; the Earth producing Metal. Since Metal represents coinage, such a situation would be financially very rewarding.

5. *Location: Earth/Structure: Water*
Earth and Water are in the destructive sequences, Water being harmed by Earth. Such a structure would not be favoured by the geomancer as its function might have an adverse effect on the neighbourhood.

Later, we shall take a closer look at each of the conditions that can arise when a building stands in a location and the element features of both buildings and location are clearly observable. Before that, however, let us look at the symbolism of each element in greater detail.

The Symbolism of Each Element

WOOD—Spring—East—Green
Material: Wood   Shape: Columnar

Although the elements follow each other in a continuous sequence, so that they have no start and no end, Wood is generally taken as the first of the series being symbolic of Spring, the beginning of the year. Consequently, Wood symbolizes creation, nourishment, and growth.

Wood environment

The Wood shape is tall and upright and is usually encountered in memorial, religious, military, or commemorative structures such as columns, obelisks, tall pagodas, watchtowers, and pillars. Until comparatively recent years, with the development of modern building techniques and the subsequent emergence of skyscrapers and tower blocks, Wood-shape structures would hardly ever be encountered for domestic or commercial use. However, Wood is a common building material, and consequently a building of standard shape might be considered to belong to the 'Wood' element if it was proposed to construct it from that material.

Buildings under the aegis of Wood would be suitable for all matters connected with creation, nourishment, and growth. Thus, nurseries, hospitals, residences, and catering establishments, as well as artists' ateliers, would benefit from the influence of the Wood element. Within a home, the dining room, the children's room and the bedroom would benefit.

In commercial premises, the Wood element, representing creativity, would be the element most suitable for the design studio, while the 'nourishing' aspect suggests that establishments connected with the victualling trades, such as restaurants, and cafés, would benefit. In manufacture and retailing, where the Wood element predominates, the production or sale of goods made from Wood is suggested.

FIRE—Summer—South—Red
Material: Plastics; animal materials   Shape: Pointed

The Fire shape is revealed by sharp angles and points, particularly of roofs, and is often found in the roofs of certain temples, such as those of Thailand, where monsoon rains make tall, sloping roofs almost mandatory, although the spires of churches are also emblematic of the Fire element. Throughout South-East Asia it is considered unlucky to build a house near a church, partly because it is thought that, since people go to church to rid themselves of evil, the evil forces are likely to take up residence in the nearest available dwelling, but also because it is thought that the close proximity of the Fire element puts wooden buildings under a constant threat of conflagration.

The fact that Fire is connected with chemical processes suggests that the Fire element rules man-made materials, although in former times no building materials—apart, perhaps, from the leather tents of the nomads—were considered as belonging to the

Fire environment

Fire element. Nevertheless, premises with sloping roofs—perhaps the commonest type of construction, whether domestic, civic, or industrial—were regarded as being of the Fire element type.

The red colour of Fire is the colour of blood, so Fire represents livestock (animal life) as distinct from vegetable life.

The Fire element is said to indicate intellect, and Fire-shaped buildings would therefore be suitable for libraries, schools, and other places of learning. In commerce, design and fashion are possibilities. More obviously, manufacturing processes involving fire and furnaces, and, less obviously, chemical processes, are categorized as belonging to the Fire element type. Livestock and (with Metal) butchery are also classed under the Fire element.

In the home, the kitchen stove is the seat of the Fire element.

EARTH—Centre—Yellow
Material: Brick   Shape: Square; flat

The Earth element is revealed by low flat buildings, flat sides, plain unadorned surfaces, and flat roofs. Blocks of flats and offices, flat-topped low buildings, and similar constructions all reveal the Earth shape.

Earth is also the element of clay and bricks, so that brick, clay, and concrete buildings have a portion of the element Earth present, whatever their shape. Thus, a brick house with a sloping roof shows both the qualities of Fire and Earth elements; since Fire and Earth stand in the generative or production order of the Five Elements, this is regarded as a stable and fortunate combination.

Buildings of a strongly 'Earth' type may be solid, enduring, and reliable, but they have no stimulating influences. Generally speaking, because they are considered to be 'immobile', their best use is for storage. In commercial premises, Earth element areas might be used for the stock-room. In the home, areas that come under the influence of the Earth element are best used for storage space, seldom-used lounges, garages or conservatories (although, strictly speaking, the latter should be in an area strongly associated with the Wood element).

In industry, the Earth element is associated with tunnelling, farming, building, and civil engineering. In commerce, the production or sale of ceramics is suggested.

Earth environment

METAL—Autumn—West—White
Material: Metal   Shape: Round

The Metal shape is revealed in buildings that have domes, curved roofs, and arches. Such buildings are nearly always of a monumental, religious, or civic nature; in the western world, domed residences tend to be confined to the palaces of the gentry, but there are countries where domed houses are the traditional form of domestic architecture.

Since Metal is the symbolic element of coinage and money, it is not surprising that so many successful commercial premises, notably banking houses, favour domed halls. In Feng Shui terms, nothing could be more appropriate for commerce than the dome shape. Those wishing for financial success, but are not yet able to afford a domed structure to roof their enterprises, may, however, content themselves with the construction of arches and other rounded ornament. Arched roofs often soar over railways stations; and it was entirely apt that this should have been the design, when railways, 'the iron roads', inaugurated a new era of trade and industry.

Today, Metal is also a component of building materials; ferroconcrete reveals a combination of the Earth and Metal elements. As Earth and Metal stand in the generative or production sequence of the Five Elements, this is regarded as fortunate—Earth produces Metal, and hence this combination of elements is said to ensure wealth and financial success.

The Metal element is more suited to commercial and manufacturing buildings than to domestic ones. Whilst Metal promises monetary gain, this element is not conducive to the simple, everyday processes of living and growing. In the home, any area that falls under the auspices of Metal should be set aside for a workshop.

The Metal element rules knives and swords. All manufacturing processes involving Metal obviously fall into the Metal category. In commercial activities, the manufacture and sale of jewellery and hardware benefit from the influence of the Metal element.

WATER—Winter—North—Black
Material: Glass   Shape: Square; flat

The Water type of building is revealed by irregularities of shape and construction. Buildings that seem thrown together, rather

Metal environment

Water environment

than designed, and seem to show features of all four of the other elements (although not too definitely angular or flat surfaced) may be said to belong to the Water element.

Water is the element of communication, and all matters concerned with the transmission of ideas will benefit from the influence of the Water element. Literature and the arts, particularly music, fall into this category, and it is perhaps a happy chance that the famous skyline of Sydney Opera House should reveal the characteristics of the Water shape most distinctively.

In modern construction, the predominant use of glass as a building material is another way in which a structure is revealed as belonging to the Water element. Glass, however, cannot be used on its own but in conjunction with some other material such as brick, metal or wood. Which of these materials is the most appropriate to use with glass, representing the Water element? Water and Earth stand in the destructive sequence; hence, it is suggested that buildings involving large expanses of glass do not benefit by having a brick support. Wood and Water, and Metal and Water, however, both stand in the generative sequences, and would therefore be much more favourable.

In the home, the obvious use of Water is for its cleaning properties, and the bathroom, laundry, and still-room are the more mundane applications of Water in its material sense. But in considering the metaphorical aspect of Water, any area that receives the beneficial influence of the Water element could appropriately be used for a study.

In business, the Water element represents post and communications, the media, advertising, word processing, computer terminology, electrical engineering, and enterprises involving liquids and fluids, such as brewing and distilling; but in the past hundred years, the oil business has now become part of the Water element's domain.

Exercise

Test your understanding of this section on the Five Elements by deciding which of the Five Elements is the one most appropriate for each of the items below. Then compare your answers with the alphabetical guide that follows:

Commerce and Industry:

Advertising ....
Artists' studios ....
Brewing ....
Building ....
Carpentry ....
Catering ....
Ceramics ....
Chemical processes ....
Civil engineering ....
Communications ....
Computers ....
Distilling ....
Electrical Engineering ....
Farming ....
Media ....
Oil industry ....
Word processing ....

Residential:

Bathroom ....
Bedroom ....
Children's room ....
Dining room ....
Garage ....
Kitchen ....
Laundry ....
Nursery ....
Storeroom ....
Workshop ....

Architectural Shapes and Features:

Angles ....
Arches ....
Blocks of flats ....
Church steeples ....
Columns ....
Curves ....
Domes ....
Flat roofs ....

Irregular shapes   . . . .
Low buildings   . . . .
Pillars   . . . .
Points   . . . .
Squares   . . . .
Tunnels   . . . .
Watchtowers   . . . .

Substances, Materials, and Objects:

Animal life   . . . .
Blood   . . . .
Bricks   . . . .
Clay   . . . .
Coinage   . . . .
Furnaces   . . . .
Furniture   . . . .
Glass   . . . .
Hardware   . . . .
Jewellery   . . . .
Knives   . . . .
Leather   . . . .
Money   . . . .
Plains   . . . .
Plants   . . . .
Pottery   . . . .
Swords   . . . .
Trees   . . . .
Vegetables   . . . .

Index to the Five Elements

Advertising—Water

Angles—Fire

Animal life—Fire

Arches—Metal

Artists' studios—Wood

Arts—Water

Bathroom—Water

Bedroom—Wood

Blocks of flats—Earth

Blood—Fire

Brewing—Water

Bricks—Earth

Building—Earth

Cafés—Wood

Carpentry—Wood
Catering establishments—Wood
Ceramics—Earth
Chemical processes—Fire
Children's room—Wood
Church steeple—Fire
Civil engineering—Earth
Clay—Earth
Coinage—Metal
Columns—Wood
Communications—Water
Computers—Water
Curves—Metal

Dining-room—Wood
Distilling—Water
Domes—Metal

Electricity—Water

Farming—Earth
Flat roofs—Earth
Furnaces—Fire
Furniture—Wood

Garages—Earth
Glass—Water
Growth—Wood

Hardware—Metal
Hospitals—Wood

Intellect—Fire
Irregular shapes—Water

Jewellery—Metal

Kitchen—Fire
Knives—Metal

Laundry—Water
Leather—Fire
Libraries—Fire
Literature—Water
Livestock—Fire
Low buildings—Earth

Media—Water
Money—Metal
Music—Water

Nourishment—Wood
Nurseries—Wood

Oil wells—Water

Pillars—Wood
Plains—Earth
Plants—Wood
Points—Fire
Post—Water
Pottery—Earth

Railways—Metal
Residences—Wood
Restaurants—Wood

Squares—Earth
Storerooms—Earth
Swords—Metal

Trees—Wood
Tunnels—Earth

Vegetables—Wood

Watchtowers—Wood
Word processing—Water
Workshop—Metal

4

The Environmental Influences on Each Type of Site

Earlier, we saw how a site (or building) was affected by the five possible types of environmental element. In practice, the site may be classified as belonging to two or more elements, but these 'compound' situations are touched upon later. For the moment, here are the Feng Shui prognostications for the five basic types of building, or 'site', within the five types of location, or 'environment'.

The Wood Site

The Wood site is a construction either made of wood, or one belonging to the Wood shape, such as a column or tower. In the following five cases, it is assumed that the building belongs purely to the Wood element, such as a wooden tower, and is not some compound structure belonging to more than one element, such as a stone column, or a wooden chalet with sharply sloping roof (signifying the Fire element).

Wood Environment/Wood Site

The Wood environment is usually revealed by neighbouring buildings being made of wood; forests and woods, or arrangements of columns for some construction.

A Wood structure in a Wood environment is stable. When the element of the environment is derived from other Wood structures, it is better for the function of the proposed structure to match those of the neighbouring buildings. If, however, the element of the environment is derived from some other feature of the landscape, perhaps a landscape of tall columnar rock shapes, the proposed building will be suitable for all matters connected with creativity, nourishment, care, or agriculture. Convalescent homes, nurseries, and horticultural centres would be expected to thrive in this kind of environment.

Fire Environment/Wood Site

The Fire environment is revealed by buildings with steep roofs, or distant mountain peaks.

Wood feeds Fire. Such a site is likely to give more to the neighbourhood than would be received; it would be better if the proposed building were to be a school or hospital—that is, something that will give to the community, rather than take from it. For this reason, commercial success is less assured. For homes, there is a danger of destruction by fire.

Earth Environment/Wood Site

The Earth environment is seen in flat plains, or by low flat-roofed buildings.

Wood destroys Earth, by taking nourishment from it and leaving it barren. This situation is the reverse of the one above, where the surroundings contribute to the welfare of the Wood building. Harnessed carefully, these circumstances could bring the occupiers great benefits, but they would only be for the short term, as eventually the favourable influences would be exhausted.

Metal Environment/Wood Site

The Metal element is symbolized by rounded hills, or by buildings with prominent domes or arches.

Metal destroys Wood. This is regarded as a potentially dangerous situation, and one which bodes accidental injury to those unfortunate enough to need to spend much of their time, either working or residing, under the influence of the malign environmental factors. Also, as Metal is the element symbolizing money, commercial premises set up here would not be likely to thrive, since the wealth of the neighbourhood would operate adversely against the personal well-being of those occupying a Wood-type building in a Metal-type environment.

Water Environment/Wood Site

The Water environment is manifested in water itself, shown by lakes, rivers, streams, and ponds, but also in buildings that have a nondescript or irregular shape.

Water produces Wood; it feeds and nourishes growth. This is consequently a very beneficial situation, one which would assure the success of all business enterprises operating in these circumstances, as well as the welfare and happiness of those who are fortunate enough to live under these favourable auspices.

The Fire Site

Fire is the element of animal life and, in human terms, of intelligence. The only building materials that can be said to be represented by Fire are those made from animal matter, or possible man-made fabrics; both types if used for construction at all, are likely to be confined to tent-like structures. Consequently, Fire-type buildings are almost exclusively those that have steeply-sloping roofs, and sharp, angular outlines.

Wood Environment/Fire Site

In a country environment, the element Wood is revealed in forests and woods; in an urban landscape, by buildings made of wood (less rarely by buildings having the typical columnar Wood shape) or by a series of posts or pillars that are part of some large-scale construction—such as a bridge, railway viaduct, or motorway.

Wood feeds Fire; hence the Fire site is nurtured by the Wood location. This is highly fortunate both for business enterprises and for residential accommodation, since in commercial activity it shows financial success, and at home, prosperity. It is said that children born to parents fortunate enough to reside in this very favourable location will be very intelligent. Given the symbolism of Fire—intellect, chemical change, and animal life—suitable enterprises cover an unusually wide field. Teaching establishments, chemical processing plants, and livestock rearing all benefit from this combination of elements.

Fire Environment/Fire Site

The Fire environment is revealed by buildings with steep roofs, sharp-angled buildings, or, in the countryside, by distant mountain peaks. Church steeples are sufficiently dominant to create an environment considered to be of the Fire type. Fire-Fire is stable and progressive. It is a beneficial combination, but very volatile; a business would thrive for a short term, but may exhaust itself after a few years. Enterprises such as fashion houses, or shops catering for the 'pop' market, would therefore be suitable activities. For a residence, the circumstances would be favourable for a first-time home, or a transit stop. Longer stays would pall after a while.

Earth Environment/Fire Site

The Earth environment is seen in flat plains, or low flat-roofed buildings. The element Earth represents the ash left by a Fire. Those who build a Fire-type house in an Earth environment will be happy with their circumstances, and will be remembered with gratitude long after they have left the area. This combination of elements is likely to be more suited to those whose highest ambitions rest in gaining the goodwill and reverence of their friends and neighbours. Those setting up in business will not become rich, but they will be respected for their honesty and integrity.

This would be an ideal situation for a hospital, school, library, or other project planned to be of benefit to the community.

Metal Environment/Fire Site

The Metal element is symbolized by rounded hills, or by buildings with prominent domes or arches. In modern times, buildings constructed of metal are now frequently found; these may be buildings with iron or steel frames, or even those with corrugated iron, zinc, or aluminium roofs. The Fire element conquers Metal; it follows that any commercial premises constructed according to the Fire shape, with pointed roofs or sharp angles, will, from the point of view of Feng Shui, have a considerable advantage over other element types. These are the circumstances that favour any enterprise determined to reap profits from the neighbourhood, and thus favour those people with ruthless business principles. For those who decide to live here, the combination of elements promises social success, and the chance to attain promotion, and political or civic office.

Water Environment/Fire Site

The Water environment is shown when water is present physically, as lakes, rivers, streams, ponds, canals, or docks, and also in buildings of irregular or indefinable shape, with an absence of bold, straight lines and angles. Water quenches Fire. It would be inadvisable therefore to set up home, or open a business, in a building that was identifiable as having the Fire shape—that is, one with sharply-sloping roofs or angles.

The Earth Site

Nowadays, buildings of the Earth type are becoming common-place; the element is represented both by flat, squarish construc-tions, which tend to be a feature favoured by architects of the latter decades of this century, and also by buildings made of 'earth', which of course includes brick and even concrete. But brick houses with sloping roofs are nevertheless, from a Feng Shui standpoint, regarded as being of the 'Fire' type, since it is prin-cipally *form* not material, that is the Feng Shui criterion when assessing the element qualities of a building.

Wood Environment/Earth Site

The Wood environment is shown either by surrounding forests of trees, or else buildings made of wood. Buildings having the typical Wood shape (tall and narrow) are unusual, but columns and pillars, as part of some large construction project, are often encountered.

Wood conquers Earth, by feeding from it. This would be an ideal situation for a couple wishing to raise a family, as they would constantly draw upon the environment for their well-being and spiritual nourishment. But just as crops exhaust the ground they grow on unless they are changed, or the ground fertilized, so eventually the goodness of the environment will be emptied by those benefiting from the Wood-type site. Commercial enterprises should aim to change their role after a few years, when the busi-ness ceases to develop. For families bringing up children in the area, plans should be made to send them away to further their education, since the environment will eventually fail to stimu-late their growth and intellectual development.

Fire Environment/Earth Site

In an urban situation, the Fire environment is seen in buildings that have sloping roofs, angles, and even triangular structures.

Mountain peaks and church steeples that dominate the skyline are also signs of the Fire type of environment.

Fire produces Earth; this is therefore a positive situation with the environment acting to the benefit of those who live or work in an Earth type of building. Both for commercial concerns, and for those living in the area, the circumstances are extremely favourable, and as the benefits are stable and continuing, this would be an ideal location for a family home or a long-term business enterprise.

Earth Environment/Earth Site

When flat-topped buildings stand in a flat plain, or among similar flat or squarish buildings, the condition is an Earth-Earth balance: an extremely stable situation, but one which is not likely to progress. These circumstances are suitable for run-of-the-mill operations, mass housing, or everyday commercial enterprises. Success is sound, but there is little room for development or expansion. The situation is neither beneficial nor harmful. To ensure the greatest stability, the function of any Earth-type structure built in an Earth-type environment should match its neighbours; in a residential area, the building should be for housing; in a commercial zone, it should be a business enterprise, and so forth.

Metal Environment/Earth Site

A flat-topped building, set among domed buildings, or surrounded by a landscape of gently-rounded hills will be at peace with its environment, but this is not the ideal situation for a commercial enterprise to thrive. Rather, these conditions are more suited to a school, or even a family home, where young people are being trained or brought up to be of service to the community in some way. If their ambitions lie with the armed forces, the police, farming, or mining, they will succeed, as they will if they decide to enter the cut and thrust of the business world. Those who decide to retire in this type of environment may find that their savings are rapidly depleted, and they will leave little inheritance.

Water Environment/Earth Site

The Water environment is one in which water is physically

present, as rivers and canals, or lakes and ponds. But buildings of an unusual shape (particularly factory buildings) that cannot be identified as one of the other four element shapes (tall, pointed, flat, or round) are often considered Water-element types.

Buildings of the Earth-element type are said to feed off their surroundings. The inhabitants of this kind of residence, or the operators of businesses, have nothing to fear but the esteem of their neighbours. Earth conquers Water; thus, while the element combination promises success, it is at the expense of the environment. It shows advancement in business and career, and heightened social standing, but not love or respect. For those people reaping the doubtful benefits of this combination, fortune will be illusory, and they will be surrounded by false friends and flatterers.

The Metal Site

The architectural shape associated with the element Metal is the circle. Buildings of the Metal type are those with prominent curved features, such as curved or semi-circular arched roofs—in particular, the Byzantine style typified by imposing domed roofs. Arched colonnades belong to the compound Wood-Metal type, the arches being a feature of the Metal element, and the pillars representing the Wood element. All these features, of course, are seldom found in humble domestic architecture but are more usually encountered in public buildings such as libraries, museums, and temples, or commercial buildings designed to display the power of the company, such as the headquarters of banks and financial houses. The latter shape is appropriate for commercial buildings, since the Metal element is not only the symbol of finance (the round shape, perhaps, suggesting coinage) but also, being the symbol of the sword, of aggressive competition.

For this reason, it is important that the directors of enterprises who are planning to erect a Metal-type building should take care that the environmental element is one that is favourable, or the commercial aspirations of the company could be shortlived.

Although the Metal shape is usually confined to grand buildings, and seldom encountered in domestic architecture, occasionally, smaller commercial buildings may be said to be represented by the element Metal, especially if the bulk of the structural material is a metal substance, such as corrugated iron sheeting, steel girders, metal roofs, and so on. Usually, such buildings are used for large-scale storage, at depots, docksides, and railway goods yards, while, on a smaller scale, general goods stores in isolated out-of-the-way country places are often constructed from whatever material is conveniently to hand, which might be metal sheeting.

It should always be remembered, however, that the Feng Shui element is principally the one which is found in the *form* rather than the structural material of the building.

Wood Environment/Metal Site

I would imagine that few readers of this book are presently contemplating the erection of a grand basilica surmounted by a magnificently gilded copper cupola, looming above either the tree-tops of some densely wooded forest, or the wooden huts of the downtrodden populace of some far-off poverty-stricken locality; yet this is the image suggested by the siting of a Metal building in a Wood environment. For since Wood, the symbol of growth and creation, is destroyed by Metal, the symbol of money and the sword, this combination of elements conjures up the picture of a despot, living richly, in his domed palace, off the taxes extorted from his oppressed subjects. Such people are unlikely to sleep less comfortably knowing that a Metal building in a Wood environment foreshadows tyranny; but perhaps for the board of a banking corporation, looking at the projected designs for their new head office, the loss of the respect and goodwill of their clients might indeed be cause for anxiety.

According to the Feng Shui principle of Metal conquering Wood, enterprises that are represented by domed buildings will flourish if the building is surrounded by a colonnaded courtyard, since the surrounding columns represent the Wood element.

At the other extreme, the humble store-keeper who sets up shop in a metal-sided shack in a village where most of the houses are wooden is likely to thrive and prosper. For the most part, however, particularly when residential use is considered, Metal-type buildings are one of the least common structural shapes to be encountered.

Fire Environment/Metal Site

Any financial organization considering constructing a domed

building for its headquarters should avoid an environment dominated by sharply-sloping roofs or peaked mountains. These represent the Fire element, which destroys Metal; consequently, the credibility and financial security of the enterprise would be at risk.

It is difficult to imagine what the residential equivalent of this element situation would be (a tin shack in the mountains?) but it is not one that would be conducive to the good financial management of the people who lived there.

Earth Environment/Metal Site

The Earth environment is one shown by a flat, unrelieved landscape, or by a neighbourhood of flat-roofed buildings. As Earth and Metal are in the generative sequence (Earth producing Metal) the situation would reveal great success for any company that chose a domed building for their headquarters in this location. Domed residential buildings are uncommon, but the family living in a home pertaining to the Metal element is destined to become rich.

Metal Environment/Metal Site

The Metal type of environment is symbolized in the countryside by rounded hills and in an urban situation by buildings with prominent domes or arches. When the element of the site is the same as the element of the surrounding environment, it is always favourable for the function of the site to match those of its neighbouring buildings. Apart from cities of the Near East and North Africa, where the domes of the whitewashed buildings help to keep the interiors cool in the intense desert heat, the Metal-Metal elemental combination is rarely encountered.

Water Environment/Metal Site

The Water environment is not only revealed by the presence of water itself, for example canals, rivers, lakes or reservoirs, but also by buildings of irregular shape.

Metal generates Water; this is an unfavourable situation for a commercial enterprise such as a finance house, since it suggests that money is continually being lost to the outside. But for a religious centre, or even a media organization (publishing, broadcasting, television), it would be ideal since it symbolizes the 'wealth' of the host organization being distributed to the world beyond.

The Water Site

Modern building techniques have considerably expanded the range of buildings that can be considered as belonging to the Water element. In the times of the sages, constructions of glass were known only in the imagination; now they are commonplace. Remember, however, that the Feng Shui element is principally the one found in the *form* of a building, rather than its structural material. Thus, the square-built glass towers that dominate the urban landscapes of so many of our cities should be regarded as manifesting both the Water and the Earth elements (two elements in the 'destructive' sequence, note), while the frightful glass pyramid at the Louvre reveals the unfortunate collaboration of the elements of both Fire and Water.

The Water shape is less easy to define because it has 'no shape, and yet every shape', but it can be recognized in buildings that have been designed and yet appear to lack the discipline of formal architecture. Outstanding examples are Gaudi's Sagrada Familia cathedral in Barcelona, or the renowned Sydney Opera House. Some might also put St Basil's Cathedral, outside the walls of the Kremlin in Red Square, Moscow, into this category too. These three buildings are renowned for their remarkable asymmetry, the crucial feature of the Water shape.

In the usual course of events, buildings pertaining to the Water element shape have usually 'grown' to their shape, through a series of extensions and developments, rather than having been designed in their present form from the outset. However, a series of straight, rectilinear figures, produced when one rectangular extension is built on to another, do not properly constitute the Water type. Notice that all three of the famous buildings described above—the Sydney Opera House, Sagrada Familia, and St Basil's—have outlines that evolve from configurations of curves.

Remember that the key to the Water type of building is primarily irregularity and asymmetry; secondly, a flowing, natural shape; and only thirdly, the use of a Water-type constructional material, such as glass.

Sometimes, because of the environment's adverse qualities, it may be important to enhance the site's Water element features, and this is often done by introducing ornamental ponds and fountains, not only outside, but also into the building itself.

In Hong Kong, visitors will notice that the larger restaurants frequently feature water gardens in the entrance lobbies; cascades of water will also be seen at the side of escalators in banking houses, or in shopping malls. The casual observer may imagine that these serve a merely ornamental purpose, but their true function is actually to enhance the positive Feng Shui aspects of the site, and to neutralize any adverse *sha*.

Wood Environment/Water Site

Water feeds Wood; the two elements are in harmony, but the neighbourhood benefits from the presence of the Water-type building. It would therefore be best if the function of a Water-type building is one that is intended to benefit the community. As Water is the symbol of the arts, music, and the media, this would be an excellent configuration of elements for a concert hall, theatre, or communications centre. The Wood environment is usually revealed by neighbouring buildings being made of wood, since few buildings have the 'Wood' shape, which is tall and columnar. In a country location, the Water type of building would be ideally suited for a centre of administration for a surrounding woodland or forest area.

Fire Environment/Water Site

The Fire element (shown by an environment of buildings with steep roofs, or else distant mountain peaks) is here destroyed by the element of the site: Water. Yet although Water is the victor, the combination of these two elements is undesirable. In a commercial undertaking, the enterprise would operate to the detriment of the surroundings. A family residing in a Water-type building would rise above their neighbours by becoming active in local politics; but their presence would be unwelcome, their concern taken as interference, and their attempts to improve the quality of life in the neighbourhood construed as a meddlesome nuisance.

Earth Environment/Water Site

It is not advisable to take up residence or employment in a Water type of building—that is, one of irregular or asymmetrical shape—that stands in an Earth-type environment, shown either by an unrelieved flat level landscape, or by surroundings that consist mostly of flat-roofed, high- or low-rise buildings. Earth and Wood are in the destructive sequence, Water being sullied or polluted by Earth. Those who spent long periods in these circumstances would be in danger of damaging their reputations, by being subject to malicious gossip, scandal, or ill-will.

Metal Environment/Water Site

When the Water type of building, of irregular but flowing shape, stands in a landscape of gently-rounded hills, representing the Metal element, or in a townscape under the protection of a building with prominent curved features such as a dome or arches, the situation is extremely favourable for both commercial and residential accommodation. Both for the business venture, as well as for the family residing in these happy circumstances, the Metal element, generating Water, reveals the accumulation of wealth and continuing prosperity.

Water Environment/Water Site

When the element of the site is the same as that of its environment, the general rule is that the function of the building on the site should match that of the other buildings round it. But this rule rarely applies in the case of the Water-type building in a Water-type environment, because Water-element buildings tend to be uncommon, and the Water-type of environment tends nearly always to refer to the physical presence of water itself. Such, for example, is the case of the Sydney Opera House, which stands conspicuously in a Water location.

The situation is both stable and flexible, maintaining continuity through the ability to make changes readily. A commercial enterprise would be able to prosper and develop successfully by being able to adapt to the changing needs of the consumer.

A Water type of house near water would see many generations of the same family raised in it, although the children born there would have great ambitions to travel. They would succeed in literature, the arts, or music and make their career in the world; but, like migratory birds, they would always yearn to return to their original home, to settle and raise their own children in the neighbourhood they loved.

Exercise

Completing the following table will help you to review the foregoing paragraphs. Decide whether the environments (indicated by the sketches along the top of the table) are regarded as beneficial, stable, or adverse for the types of buildings shown in the left hand column of the table. You can check your opinions with the completed table that follows.

Environment / Site					
Wood					
Fire					
Earth					
Metal					
Water					

| Site Element | *Environmental Element* | | | | |
	WOOD	FIRE	EARTH	METAL	WATER
Wood	□	▼	▲	■	*
Fire	*	□	▼	▲	■
Earth	■	*	□	▼	▲
Metal	▲	■	*	□	▼
Water	▼	▲	■	*	□

Key: □ *Stable*   ▼ *Weak*   ▲ *Unhappy*   ■*Danger*   *Ideal

Controlling Elements

When a building belongs to an element group that is in a location harmful to it—for example, if a Wood-type building is set in Metal-type surroundings—the adverse effects may be rectified by introducing a *controlling* element into the situation.

A controlling element can either be the one that destroys the harmful element, or else generates the element under threat. Thus, in the case above, where Wood was under threat from Metal, the situation could be remedied by introducing a factor representing either Water, which produces Wood, or Fire, which destroys Metal.

The charts on pp. 79-81 indicate when each element may be considered to be under threat, and how such situations may be rectified by the introduction of a third element.

Buildings of Two Elements

We have seen that some buildings may already be considered to be of two element factors: for example, buildings of Wood with pointed (Fire-type) roofs; buildings of ferro-concrete, representing both Metal and Earth; and buildings of glass (Water element) and some other construction material, whether wood, metal, or brick. Such buildings may blend harmoniously with their surroundings if the three elements followed each other in the production sequence, or if they are mutually balanced because the controlling element was either present in the constructional materials of the building's fabric, or was the element of the location.

Introducing the Controlling Element

When the environmental element is considered to be harmful to the element of the site, some means of introducing a controlling element has to be found.

One of the commonest Feng Shui remedies to be encountered is to have a bowl of goldfish in a room opposite a window which looks out on to a column, telegraph pole, lamp-post, or other kind of pillar. An odd number of goldfish is usually stipulated by the Feng Shui master, and the colour of the fish is invariably red, symbolizing Fire. The explanation given is that the premises being under threat by the Wood element, the red fish in the water represent the elements Fire and Water. Since the three elements Water, Wood, and Fire follow each other in the generative sequence, the three elements are consequently in harmony and the danger is quelled.

In a simple case, where both the location and the site are represented by single elements, and the site element is under threat from a potentially dangerous environmental element, some appropriate means must be found of introducing the third element. Feng Shui consultants vary tremendously in the kind of advice they might give their clients; and the remedies range just as much in their appropriateness, practicality, and cost. The third (controlling element) might be symbolized by its Feng Shui colour, its substance, or shape. There is no limit to the imaginative processes given these few factors. Actual suggestions showing how each element may be represented are given in a later section of this book.

The reader should try to become more familiar with the principle of the 'controlling elements' by completing the tables at the end of this section, using the charts given here. It must be emphasized that there will be numerous references to the generative and destructive sequences in this book, and readers who become conversant with the sequences now will find it much easier to understand later chapters.

Example of Controlling Elements (1)

(a) is under threat from (b); (c) is the controlling element by virtue of the fact that it destroys the threatening element.

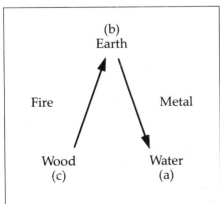
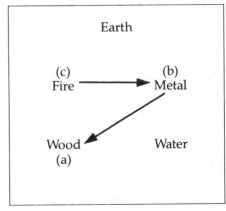

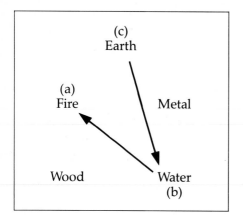

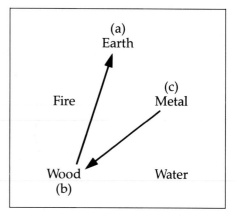

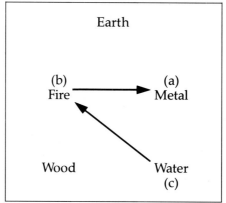

Example of Controlling Elements (2)

(a) is under threat from (b); (c) is the controlling element by virtue of the fact that it generates the element under threat.

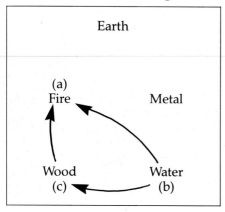

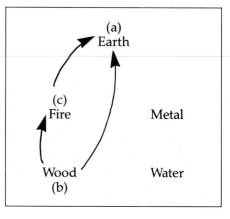

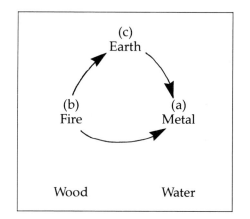

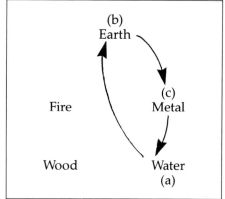

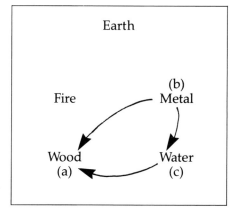

Exercise

You may like to practise your understanding of the preceding section by completing the following chart. You can then compare your completed chart with the key that follows.

ELEMENT of the SITE	THREATENING ELEMENT	CONTROLLING ELEMENT *either* *or*
WOOD	Metal	Fire Water
FIRE		
EARTH		
METAL		
WATER		

KEY

ELEMENT of the SITE	THREATENING ELEMENT	CONTROLLING ELEMENT	
		either	*or*
WOOD	METAL	FIRE	WATER
FIRE	WATER	EARTH	WOOD
EARTH	WOOD	METAL	FIRE
METAL	FIRE	WATER	EARTH
WATER	EARTH	WOOD	METAL

5

The Interior of the Site: The Trigrams and the Auspices

We now approach one of the most intriguing aspects of Feng Shui: the locating of fortunate areas within the building and the detection of unfavourable situations that are best avoided. With regard to a residence, whether a mansion or a family home, we shall find those parts, be they rooms or merely divisions of a room, that are best suited for sleeping, dining, or working in. We shall identify those areas that are deemed to harbour unfortunate influences, and which are therefore to be avoided, or at best used for storage, and even those areas that are reputedly haunted and might be used for those with mediumistic powers to call upon the spirits of their ancestors!

In respect of the office or the workplace, it will be possible to identify which areas are the ones most suitable for manufacturing, packaging, or despatch; or indeed, which areas might, for example, be liable to bring injury to employees, and those places regarded as being prone to fire.

This is obviously a major step forward in our study of Feng Shui, and not surprisingly it requires a somewhat deeper understanding of Chinese philosophical principles. Before we get involved in the details, let us look at the broad outlines of what is involved.

Matching the Site to the Environment

We have already seen one way in which the environment affects the site when we considered the effect of the elements of the environment on those of the site. We were principally concerned with *shapes and forms*, because we were following the precepts of the Form School of Feng Shui.

Now it is the turn of the Compass School to advise on the relation of the environment to the site. In this respect, we now look at the orientation of the site (in other words, the directions faced by the front, back, and sides of the building under consideration) and compare this with the orientation of the environment, or, more simply, its relation to geographical north (or, as the Chinese would have it, south. The Chinese formerly printed their maps with south at the top—and why not? South, representing warmth, prosperity, and abundance, is a much more positive direction than the cold, bleak, windy north, so it would seem logical to place south in the exalted position.)

Perhaps on this point it is worth pointing out that during my travels in China I made careful enquiry from practising geomancers to find out whether they preferred to use a true geographical north-south alignment, or the variable magnetic north-south. All my informants told me emphatically that they used the magnetic north-south alignment as their base line; but that does not mean that there may not be other geomancers practising today (or even geomancers in the past) who would prefer to use a true north-south alignment based on observation of the Sun's position at noon.

Comparison of Form School and Compass School Methods

By studying the observations of the site made according to the principles of the Form School, we are able to compile opinions on the suitability of building in that particular place, and even the style of architecture that would be most appropriate for whatever future function the building is to have. Next, following the Compass School's observations, we will be able to decide, after studying the orientation of the building, what is the ideal allocation of the interior space.

The Site Within the Location

You will remember that the Four Directions, East, South, West, and North, are known by the four astronomical animals, Dragon, Bird, Tiger, and Tortoise. At the same time, these four animals are also applied to the right side, front, left side, and back of a site.

Thus, for the most part, there will be one 'Dragon' position for the location, and another for the site. This section introduces the effect of orientation (the direction faced by the front) of the site, within the actual location.

Firstly, a word about the Dragon of the location. It is rare to find the ideal place to build, even if purchasing funds are limitless. It would be excellent to find a place with a dramatic Dragon poised on the east side, and a less prominent hill on the west, nestling in the protective Dragon's embrace. To the north will be a grove of tall conifers, or a snow-capped mountain in the distance, and a splendid lake to the south, on the shore of which, not too far from the building, is a single tall rock, of agreeable appearance, representing the Bird of the South.

Lower down the scale, there can be a variety of locations more or less advantageously situated. For example, an average location might have no Dragon, Tortoise, or Bird, but a beneficial Tiger, while right at the bottom of the ladder would be the worst kind of urban locality, with no beneficial Feng Shui features whatsoever and bristling with malevolent secret arrows surrounded by a host of adverse *sha*-generating edifices.

If the Feng Shui of the site is itself beneficial, then a well-defined Dragon, Bird, Tortoise, and Tiger in the location will increase the beneficial aspects of those parts of the site that receive the location's *ch'i*. If, on the other hand, the site is generally inauspicious, perhaps because there is a lack of *ch'i* but an abundance of *sha*, then certain unfavourable aspects of the site can be eradicated by the location's favourable position.

But the reasoning by which the sages of old calculated which directions were the most favourable when a site was oriented within a location are extremely complex, and not at all as straightforward as one might expect. Such philosophical arguments need not detain the 'practical' Feng Shui student, however. Rather, it is the application of the methods used by Feng Shui practitioners that are of greater interest, and for this reason we should look next at the effect of the eight possible orientations (that is, North, North-east, East, South-east, South, South-west, West and North-west) on the interior functioning of a Site.

So far, we have only looked at the four principal directions, North, East, South, and West. To these we now add what are called by the Chinese the 'four corners':

North-west	North	North-east
West		East
South-west	South	South-east

Chinese compasses invariably designate the eight points of the compass by special signs known as 'trigrams', but before discussing how the 'Eight Trigrams' are allocated to the eight points of the compass (since there is more than one method!) we first need to know something about the 'Eight Trigrams' themselves.

The Eight Trigrams

The Eight Trigrams are sacred emblems—they appear on the national flag of South Korea, for example, just as a cross or a crescent appears on the flags of other countries. The symbols are said to have been borne on the back of a celestial animal which rose from the deep at the beginning of time. They are considered to encapsulate the secrets of the universe. In fact, since they represent in miniature the binary system of mathematics, now an indispensable part of modern scientific thought, the legend has a strange relevance today.

The eight symbols consist of three horizontal lines, which may be either broken, thus ■ ■ , or unbroken, thus ■ . The broken lines ■ ■ are called *yin* lines, and the unbroken ones ■ *yang*.

There are eight possible permutations of three *yin* and *yang* lines. Each of them has a special Chinese name. Because the names are very ancient it is not possible in every case to give an accurate translation of the Chinese name. Even Chinese scholars often dispute the actual meanings of the names, because the words are now used in modern Chinese with a rather different usage (just as some English words used today would have been understood entirely differently a hundred years ago, let alone two thousand years or more). Here are the Eight Trigrams and their names:

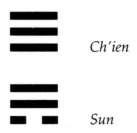

Ch'ien

Sun

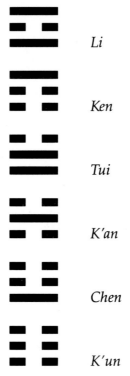

Li

Ken

Tui

K'an

Chen

K'un

Unfortunately, there is no getting away from the fact that, to the western ear, the names of the trigrams are disconcertingly similar, while the patterns of lines (at least for the moment) are remarkable only for their lack of distinguishing characteristics. But it will soon be discovered that each of these patterns has a life and individuality of its own. Because of this, the student who is able to memorize the eight names, and apply them to the appropriate trigrams unhesitatingly, will be at a decided advantage when proceeding through later sections of this book.

Exercise

To stimulate the reader's retention of the names of the trigrams, the following preliminary exercises will be found useful.

1. Name the missing trigrams:

(a) *K'an   Ken   Ch'ien   Chen   Sun   K'un   Li*   ....

(b) *K'an   Sun   Ken   K'un   Chen   Tui   Ch'ien* ....
(c) *K'an   Ken   Chen   Sun   Li   Kun* ....
(d) *K'an   Ch'ien   Tui   K'un   Li   Sun* ....
(e) *K'an   Ken   K'un   Sun*....   ....

2. Name these trigrams:

(a)

(b)

(c)

(d)

(e)

Answers

1.   (a) *Tui* (b) *Li* (c) *Ch'ien, Tui* (d) *Chen, Ken*
     (e) *Ch'ien, Chen, Tui, Li*

2.   (a) *Ch'ien, K'un, Li, K'an*
     (b) *Sun, Tui, Ken, Chen*
     (c) *Li, K'un, Sun, Tui*
     (d) *Ch'ien, Sun, Li, Ken*
     (e) *Chen, K'un, Tui, K'an*

Understanding the Trigrams

Perhaps the most memorable of the patterns are the four shown in example (a) of Exercise 2 above. These are the three complete lines [☰] *Ch'ien*, the three broken lines [☷] *K'un*, the two complete lines enclosing a broken one [☲] *Li*, and the two broken lines enclosing a complete one [☵] *K'an*. You will soon discover that these have an important role to play in Feng Shui calculations.

Let us try and identify these four trigrams in some way.

You will recall that the complete lines are *yang*, with masculine attributes, while the broken lines are *yin* with feminine attributes. *Ch'ien* [☰] with three complete lines, and therefore the most strongly *yang*, can, therefore be considered the Father trigram; conversely, *K'un* [☷] the most *yin* trigram, represents the Mother.*

Now consider the other two 'principal' trigrams, *Li* and *K'an*. *Li* has two *yang* lines enclosing a *yin* one. Think of this as Heaven's power (which is considered to be *yang*) embracing the Earth, and since Heaven's powers are manifested by the sun, which is at its greatest strength in the south, *Li* therefore represents the sun, heat, and the southern direction. Conversely, by the same reasoning, since the *K'an* trigram is the opposite of *Li*, it must represent cold and the north.

In a similar fashion, each of the eight trigrams is believed to have its own particular symbolism, meaning, and effect. Chinese philosophy teaches that all things, material or abstract, can be reduced to a formula of *yin* or *yang*. Is it just theory? The greatest music, through digital recordings, is now perfectly reproduced by means of positive or negative pulses; computers, similarly, through the binary system, deal with inestimably complex problems by reducing them to a succession of plus or minus impulses. Even human thought is created by means of positive and negative electrical charges through the neurons of the brain. Thus it is that the Eight Trigrams are regarded as the primary building bricks of the universe.

The three lines of each trigram are counted from the bottom upwards, and as the lowest line is the base it follows that those trigrams that have a complete line at the bottom are regarded as being more stable than those with a *yin* line at the bottom. Thus,

*The similarity of the word *K'un* to an English vulgarism is unlikely to be a coincidence. It probably shares the same ancient origins as the Greek *gune*, 'woman', and the Latin *cunnus*, 'vulva'. Basic 'primitive' words seem to be common to all languages: note the Chinese words for mother and father: *mu* and *fu*.

when one trigram encounters another, the result will either incline towards greater stability or towards movement and change.

We have already had a brief look at the way that the symbolism of four of the Eight Trigrams has been derived. Later, when we start to assess the Feng Shui of a site, we will need to be familiar with the symbolism of each of the Eight Trigrams in greater detail. Firstly, however, we need to know which trigram applies to each of the Eight Directions.

The Directions of the Trigrams

Those readers with a mathematical turn of mind will know that the number of possible arrangements of the Eight Trigrams is *8!* ($1 \times 2 \times 3 \times 4 \times 5 \times 6 \times 7 \times 8$), or 40,320. Of these, the most logical sequence might seem to be one which began with *K'un* (three open lines) and ended with *Ch'ien* (three complete lines). The Chinese sages of old, however, had other views, principally because if the Eight Trigrams were arranged round a dial in this order *K'un* and *Ch'ien* would be next to each other: an incongruity.

Instead, two sequences were favoured, one known as the 'Former Heaven' sequence, the other the 'Later Heaven' sequence. The 'Former Heaven' sequence is usually found on talismans and mirrors designed to ward off evil *sha*. However, it is the 'Later Heaven' sequence that is found on the dials of Chinese mariners' compasses.

We saw earlier that two of the trigrams, *K'an* and *Li*, could be thought of as North and South respectively, and in fact are found in those positions on the dials of compasses. Now it might be thought that the most logical trigrams to be allocated to the North and South positions would be the two trigrams of three similar lines: *K'un*, the three broken lines, representing the North, and *Ch'ien*, with three complete lines, representing the South. This is in fact the case with the 'Former Heaven' sequence used for talismans. But, partly for the reasoning outlined above, and more particularly because of certain passages in the *I Ching** (regarded as a sacred text), *Ch'ien* and *K'un* are always considered to represent the North-West and South-West directions respectively.

The two arrangements of the Eight Trigrams are:

*See Hexagram II, 'K'un'.

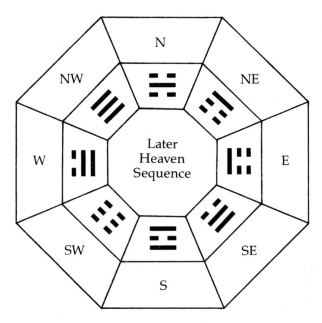

The Later Heaven Sequence

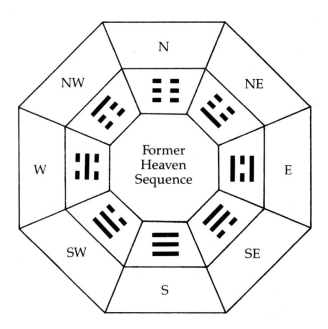

The Former Heaven Sequence

In the Later Heaven Sequence, trigrams are *not* the converse of their opposite partners. (The trigrams are read from the inside, outwards.)

Note that in the Former Heaven Sequence, each diagram is the converse of the one opposite.

The Trigrams and Feng Shui

The fact that there are two sequences reveals that while it is almost true to say that there is a standard position for each of the trigrams, these positions are not absolutely fixed. But the names of the trigrams remain unchanged, and, with their names, the symbolism for each trigram also remains the same, wherever it appears. The trigram of three unbroken lines will always be *Ch'ien*, and it will always be the symbol of the creative, the male, and Heaven, while the three broken lines will always be *K'un*, representing the nourishing, female, and Earth. And according to the symbolism, the most appropriate form of activity (on the domestic level, for example, eating, sleeping, work, studying, cooking, storage, and so on) can be selected to take place in the area of the site occupied by each trigram. Similarly, in business premises, different areas will be allocated to the design, manufacture, ordering, selling, storage, and despatch goods.

In addition to ruling various spheres of activity, the trigrams also pertain to family relationships. We have already seen that the *Ch'ien* and *K'un* trigrams are the Father and Mother trigrams. If we look at the *Li* trigram, we see that the middle line is a *yin* or feminine line; this is a reminder that *Li* represents the 'middle' daughter; a female who is neither the youngest nor eldest in the family. By the same token, *K'an*, which has a unbroken line in the middle, with two *yin* lines either side, represents the middle son; a male, who again, is neither the youngest nor the eldest in the family.

We can now look at the symbolism of each of the Eight Trigrams.

TRIGRAM	SYMBOL	FAMILY RELATION- SHIP	QUALITY	FORMER HEAVEN SEQUENCE	LATER HEAVEN SEQUENCE	ELEMENT
☰ *Ch'ien*	Heaven	Father	Authority	S	NW	Metal
☴ *Sun*	Wind	Eldest Daughter	Growth, Trade	SW	SE	Wood
☲ *Li*	Heat	Middle Daughter	Fire	E	S	Fire
☶ *Ken*	Mountain	Youngest Son	Obstacles	NW	NE	Earth
☱ *Tui*	Sea	Youngest Daughter	Joy	SE	W	Metal
☵ *K'an*	Lake	Middle Son	Wheels, Danger	W	N	Water
☳ *Chen*	Thunder	Eldest Son	Speed, Roads	NE	E	Wood
☷ *K'un*	Earth	Mother	Nourish- ment	N	SW	Earth

Exercises

What qualities are associated with these trigrams?

Example: Ch'ien ☰ Authority

(a) ☵

(b) ☲

(c) ☷

(d) ☶

What trigrams are associated with these qualities?

Example: Joy *Tui* ☱

(a) Authority

(b) Nourishment

(c) Fire

(d) Obstacles

Complete this chart according to the Later Heaven Sequence. (In these examples, the trigrams are read from the centre, outwards, the bottom lines being those closest to the middle.)

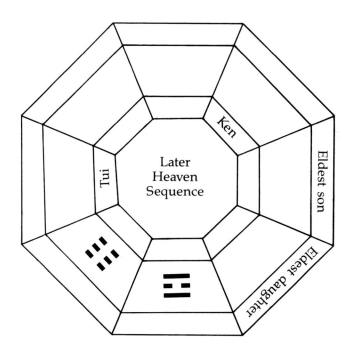

Complete this talismanic arrangement of the Eight Trigrams according to the Former Heaven Sequence.

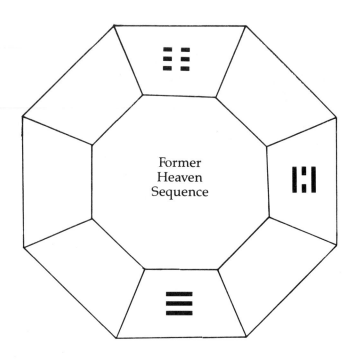

The Eight Orientations

In the Compass School of Feng Shui, buildings are classified according to one of eight principal types, depending on the direction faced by the main door. Buildings that are not in alignment with one of the Eight Directions are classified according to the nearest direction. Later in this book we shall take a closer look at the Chinese compass plate, which will enable us to decide which orientation should be chosen for buildings facing directions in between the Eight Directions, such as SSE or ESE. For the time being, however, we should content ourselves by keeping to the eight principal orientations.

In Feng Shui nomenclature, the eight types of orientations of a building are known by their respective trigram names, according to the Later Heaven Sequence. The following diagram will remind the reader of the eight trigram names.

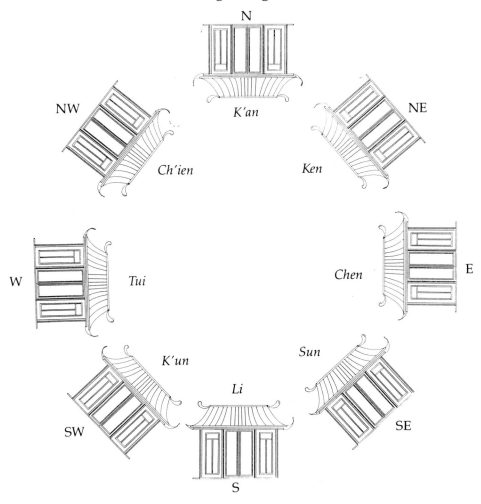

The Auspices

We can imagine the floor-plan of the building to be divided into nine, like this:

The eight outer divisions, or rooms, might then each be allocated a trigram, according to the direction faced by the building,
with the entrance, of course, at its relevant compass direction.
The central division does not face any direction, and in any case
in traditional Chinese buildings would have been a courtyard;
thus from a directional point of view, none of the trigrams is relevant to it.

The Compass School of Feng Shui explains that the interior of
any building will have places that are intrinsically more favourable than others, just as, conversely, there are areas that could
be detrimental to the well-being of any person living or working
there for long periods. Why such areas should be beneficial or
adverse has nothing to do with the lighting, physical security,
ventilation, furnishings, or whatever, but depends on the orientation of the building within its environment.

In former times, the *Book of Rites*, one of the sacred Chinese
classics, dictated which rooms of the palace should be occupied
by the Emperor at each season and month of the year. As the
Emperor's palace always faced south, these precepts were the
foundation for the ritual distribution of correct and incorrect divisions of the residences of lesser ranking persons, who were unable
to enjoy the advantage of facing the south.

Ancient sages calculated whether various areas were favourable or not according to the results obtained when the trigrams
of the Former Heaven sequence were imposed upon those of the
Later Heaven sequence and whether the resulting conjunctions
of trigrams were harmonious or otherwise.

The fortunate regions of the interior of a house or building are
known by particular names:

Nien Yen	Lengthened Years
Sheng Ch'i	Generating Breath
T'ien I	Celestial Monad

as are the unfavourable regions:

Hai Huo	Accident and Mishap
Chüeh Ming	Severed Fate
Wu Kuei	Five Ghosts
Liu Sha	Six Curses

The remaining area is the one pertaining to the entrance. The
area corresponding to the entrance, as say on an upper floor, is

considered to be neither favourable nor unfavourable.

Thus, the conjunctions of the trigrams for each direction of the environment with those of the building itself result in the seven 'portents' listed above (or eight portents, if the entrance is included).

The way that the portents apply to each direction does not follow a pattern that is immediately apparent, since they derive from the interaction of the Former and Later sequences. The reader should study the following chart carefully, noting the peculiarities of the 'migration' of the seven portents. It is not necessary to memorize this chart, however; it is repeated later in this book at a convenient point.

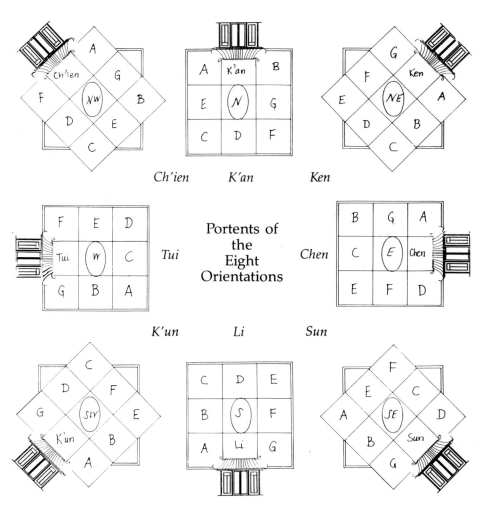

Ch'ien   K'an   Ken

Tui   Portents of the Eight Orientations   Chen

K'un   Li   Sun

The key to the distribution of the Seven Portents is taken from their order in the fundamental 'South' arrangement of the *Li* type of building.

The Eight Directions and their Portents

1. The South-facing or *Li* type of building.

2. The South-west-facing or *K'un* type of building.

3. The West-facing or *Tui* type of building.

4. The North-west-facing or *Ch'ien* type of building.

5. The North-facing or *K'an* type of building.

6. The North-east-facing or *Ken* type of building.

7. The East-facing or *Chen* type of building.

8. The South-east-facing or *Sun* type of building.

KEY LETTER	PORTENT
A	Six Curses
B	Five Ghosts
C	Severed Fate
D	Lengthened Years
E	Accident and Mishap
F	Generating Breath
G	Celestial Monad
H	(*The direction faced by the building*)

The Portents

(A) *Six Curses.* This area appears to be known by other titles, such as the Seven Imps or the Seventh Curse. In astrology, it derives its name from the fact that it is seven stars away from the natal star. It portends an event—even though it may only be a minor setback—that one has cause to regret seven times.

(B) *Five Ghosts.* The Five Ghosts are departed spirits of people who once lived on the Earth, as distinct from non-human supernatural beings such as the Seven Imps, above. It follows that this area will have a 'haunted' quality to it. It may be reserved for a memorial table to one's ancestors, a table for family photographs, or a household shrine to protect the premises. Such a room would ideally be used by mediums for communication with the departed spirits.

(C) *Severed Fate*. This refers to the ending of life, a most inauspicious situation for the bedroom of a sick person. It would be better to use this area for storage. Some Chinese apartments or buildings are deliberately constructed with one corner cut off— the 'missing corner' being the one corresponding to this unfavourable portent.

(D) *Lengthened Years*. This area, as its name suggests, has the opposite aspect to that of the one preceding. This would be an ideal area for living, working, or sleeping. The principal bedroom might be placed here.

(E) *Accident and Mishap*. This area is vulnerable to accidents bringing physical injury. Every care should therefore be taken to ensure all safety precautions are constantly reviewed. An area best reserved, perhaps, for storage, or the minimum of activity. It would be very unwise for the kitchen, bathroom, or children's bedroom to occupy this spot, knowing the inherent dangers.

(F) *Generating Breath*. This area is full of energizing vitality. It should be harnessed so that its beneficial forces are channelled to best advantage. It may be used as a work room, or study, or any room where long periods are spent. An ideal location for the creative worker's studio.

(G) *Celestial Monad*. This is a favourable location, and as it is said to neutralize malign powers it should be used by those who have experienced some kind of ill fortune or suffering and feel the need for regeneration, either physically, mentally, spiritually, or even financially.

(H) *The Direction faced by the building*. The auspices here are favourable. For an upper floor, a room situated over the entrance would be suitable for a study or a spare bedroom.

Whether it should be used by any particular member of the household is something that might be decided by reference to the Table of Relationships of the Eight Trigrams (see p. 109). In a later chapter, however, we shall see how a person's horoscope can be matched with the orientation of the house, and the neutral aspects of the Entrance Direction will be considered again.

Exercises

How would a Feng Shui consultant deal with these cases? The answers are all contained in the previous section. Once you have made up your mind, compare your findings with those given at the end of this section.

1. A family have moved into a north-facing house, and for this reason have put their principal bedroom at the back. Is this a good idea?

2. Mr Lang has a house with an entrance facing east. There is a kitchen to the west of the house and a storeroom in the south-west corner. Mrs Lang would like to extend the kitchen by converting the storeroom. Is it advisable?

3. The entrance to the Lees' house faces south-west. There are small reception/cloakrooms on each side of the entrance, one of which Mr Lee would like to use for his office and study. Which would be the more suitable?

4. The Chang family are traditionalist Chinese who have just moved into a small flat of the *Tui* type, for which practically all space has been allocated. They wish to erect a small shrine at a convenient spot. Advise.

5. Mr James' elderly mother occasionally comes to visit. There is a spare bedroom on the upper floor over the north-west-facing entrance hall. Would this be suitable?

Reasoning

1. The back of the north-facing *K'an* type of house is the south. Turning to the *K'an* diagram on p. 101, we see the letter D in the south position. From the key we see that D represents Lengthened Years, ideally suited for the main bedroom.

2. The east-facing or *Chen* type of house has the present kitchen in position C and the store-room in position E. These correspond to Severed Fate, and Accident and Mishap respectively. If Mrs Lang does decide to extend the kitchen, the greatest care must be taken concerning the installation of any equipment, and every consideration given to safety precautions at all times.

3. To the right of the entrance in the south-aligned cloakroom is the portent A, Six Curses, and to the left, in the west-aligned small receiving room, is the portent G, Celestial Monad. In the south-facing room, a study might be subject to continual minor interruptions and irritations; on the other hand, a more creative atmosphere could be felt in the west-facing room. The better would therefore be the west-facing room to the left of the entrance.

4. The most appropriate location for a household shrine would be at the portent Five Ghosts, which in the *Tui*-type of building (west-facing) is at position B (due south).

5. The area above the entrance in a multi-storied building is neither beneficial nor harmful, and so may be readily used as a spare bedroom.

6

Matching Home and Horoscope

We now turn to another intriguing facet of Feng Shui: how a home may be oriented to fit the personality of the person living in it, revealed by a special 'Feng Shui' horoscope compiled for that person.

The Feng Shui horoscope reveals the directions that are most suitable for a particular individual. Thus, it may be that a house which faces a certain direction may be generally more favourable for one person than for another. When the portents for a particular house are calculated, it may be that rooms defined as unfavourable may be the very ones that are fortunate for the person thinking of living there; on the other hand, those rooms which, because of the building's orientation, are regarded as energizing and stimulating may be the very ones the prospective occupier must avoid.

Therefore, it is necessary to compile lists of data—one for the house, another for the prospective occupier—and compare them. From this information it is possible to make a more finely-tuned assessment of the building's potential for its prospective occupier. Some buildings may be ideal for one person, but not for another.

In China, it is customary for the Feng Shui horoscope to be that of the head of the family; even today, in Chinese terms this means the father or husband. But there is no reason at all why the horoscope should not be that of a lady, if she is the head of the family. Better still, however, is the calculation that takes into account the horoscopes of both the husband and wife, or both partners in a joint relationship. The calculations are no different, and it is a fascinating exercise to see how rooms or areas that may be suitable for one partner are not appropriate for the other; or, in other cases, how both sets of calculations are compatible.

(To forestall any possible disappointment later, what is meant here by a 'Feng Shui Horoscope' is merely a set of calculations that enable the geomancer to assess what is the most favourable direction, for travel or residence, based on a person's birth date; it is not a 'character reading' such as might be expected of an astrological horoscope!)

In this following section, we shall first look at some aspects of the Chinese calendar on which the Feng Shui horoscope is based. Then we shall go through the calculations step by step. They are not too complicated, and the reader should not find that these pose any difficulty. After that, we shall see how the horoscope of the individual, or partners, can be compared with the portents of the building itself.

The Rule of Nine and the *Lo Shu*

Central to the understanding of the Feng Shui horoscope is the Rule of Nine. This is the observation—found, too, in western numerology—that all numbers can be reduced, by adding their digits, to a single digit, 1 to 9.

Chinese numerology is very ancient, and references to it can be found in texts written at least as early as the second century BC, for example in the *Book of the Prince of Huai Nan* and, more extensively, in commentaries to the *I Ching* that date from the sixth century. Manuscripts found in the monasteries of Tun Huang that date from the eighth century show ample evidence for the important ritual significance of nine-figure numerology. Legend, however, puts the discovery of nine-figure numerology back to the dawn of time, with the sage Fu Hsi finding a magic square of nine numbers (in which every row, horizontal, vertical, and diagonal, adds up to the same figure: 15) in the markings of a tortoise that emerged from the River Lo. For this reason,

S

4	9	2
3	5	7
8	1	6

E (left of table)   W (right of table)

N

the magic square is known to the Chinese as the *Lo Shu*, the (River) Lo Book.

Each of these numbers, except 5, faces one of the Eight Directions; it follows, therefore, that every number from 1 to 9 may be associated with one of the eight secondary compass points, and, as a result, with one of the Eight Trigrams.

Firstly let us remind ourselves of the names of the trigrams associated with each direction, and from the diagram above, note its relevance *Lo Shu* number; then we can list the trigrams in order of their *Lo Shu* number.

Thus from this table:

North	*K'an*	1	
North-east	*Ken*	8	
East	*Chen*	3	
South-east	*Sun*	4	
South	*Li*	9	
South-west	*K'un*	2	
West	*Tui*	7	
North-west	*Ch'ien*	6	

we can derive the following:

North	*K'an*	1	
South-west	*K'un*	2	
East	*Chen*	3	
South-east	*Sun*	4	
Centre		5	
North-west	*Ch'ien*	6	
West	*Tui*	7	
North-east	*Ken*	8	
South	*Li*	9	

Without the *Lo Shu* as the key, the numbers associated with the Eight Trigrams might appear to run in a random order, while, conversely, there may appear to be no logical sequence for the numbers associated with each direction.

In the Feng Shui calendar, all Chinese dates—the years, months, days and even the hours themselves—may be reduced to a single digit. So by pursuing the correspondence between the numbers, the Eight Directions, and the Eight Trigrams further, each aspect of the date can then be shown to have its relevant trigram and particular direction.

The Chinese Calendar

The Chinese calendar is an extremely complex one. Unlike the western calendar, with a year of fixed length, the Chinese calendar is lunar; that is, one in which every month begins with the New Moon. The Chinese New Year itself begins with the second New Moon after the Winter Solstice (the shortest day, usually 21 or 22 December) and because of this tends to vary from somewhere in the middle of January to the middle of February. A further complication for the Chinese Feng Shui consultant is that the lunar calendar then has to be converted to a solar one (that is, one that uses the sun's course through the sky as its measuring stick), because Feng Shui calculations are based on the solar year.

But now some fortunate news. Western Feng Shui students have a tremendous advantage over their Chinese counterparts, for the simple reason that the western calendar is already a solar one. This means that it only takes a few steps to find the relevant Feng Shui number from the western date. Very occasionally, when a date is a borderline case, it will be necessary to look more closely at the calendar tables in the appendix; but in most cases the conversion will be straightforward, needing only a simple formula.

The Year

The Chinese lunar year begins with the second New Moon after the Winter Solstice; but there is another, older calendar called the 'Farmer's Calendar', founded on the sun's position. The Farmer's Calendar divides the year into twenty-four 'solar fortnights' (each approximately fifteen days long), two of which make a 'solar month'. The exact moments of the Spring Equinox, the Summer Solstice, the Autumn Equinox, and the Winter Solstice, are the mid-points of the second, fifth, eighth, and eleventh months respectively. From this, it will be seen that the Chinese regard these four calendar markers not, as we do, as the beginning of each season, but the mid-points. For example, while we consider the Spring Equinox (usually 21 March) as the beginning of Spring, for the Chinese it is the middle of Spring. That means that the Chinese beginning of Spring falls around 4 February, which date is consequently the beginning of the Chinese Farmer's Calendar, or Solar Year. For the present, we only need to know of the twelve solar months, but in a later section there will be a reference to the twenty-four 'solar fortnights'. Readers who are familiar with western astrology may have noticed that the solar months virtually coincide with the twelve zodiacal signs, except that it is the latter half of one solar month, and the first half of the following one, which together complete one sign of the zodiac.

For those readers interested in comparing the Chinese solar months with the zodiacal signs they are listed here, together with the names of the twenty-four solar fortnights.

APPROXIMATE DATE	SOLAR FORTNIGHT	ZODIACAL SIGN
4 Feb	1 Spring Begins	[Aquarius]
	2 Rain Water	Pisces
6 Mar	3 Insects Waken	
	4 Spring Equinox	Aries
6 Apr	5 Clear and Bright	
	6 Corn Rain	Taurus
6 May	7 Summer Begins	
	8 Corn Sprouting	Gemini
6 June	9 Corn in Ear	
	10 Summer Solstice	Cancer
7 July	11 Little Heat	
	12 Great Heat	Leo
8 Aug	13 Autumn Begins	
	14 Heat Ends	Virgo
8 Sept	15 White Dew	
	16 Autumn Equinox	Libra
9 Oct	17 Cold Dew	
	18 Frost Descends	Scorpio
8 Nov	19 Winter Begins	
	20 Little Snow	Sagittarius
7 Dec	21 Great Snow	
	22 Winter Solstice	Capricorn
6 Jan	23 Little Cold	
	24 Great Cold	Aquarius

The essential data of this table are repeated later, at a convenient point.

Calculating the Feng Shui Horoscope Number

We are now able to calculate a person's Feng Shui Horoscope number (which, for convenience, in future we shall call the Natal Number) and from this, find out which directions are the most appropriate.

There are four stages.

1. Find the Annual Number. This is the number that corresponds with the year in which the person was born. This will be explained shortly.

2. Find the Solar Month in which the person was born. In the majority of cases, this can be done directly by reference to the table on p.111.

3. Find the Natal Number. This is done simply by cross-referring the Annual Number with the Solar Month in the Table of Natal Numbers below.

4. Every Natal Number has its appropriate trigram, direction, and element. The most harmonious place in a building is the one whose ruling element generates the element associated with the person's Natal Number.

Stages 2 and 3 above should be straightforward enough, but the first and fourth stages obviously need further clarification.

To Find the Annual Number

In the Compass School of Geomancy, as in Nine Number numerology, every year has its own number, from 1 to 9. These run in reverse order, changing each year on the date 'Spring Begins'. From 1981 to the end of the century, 'Spring Begins' is always 4 February; before 1981 'Spring Begins' may occur on 4 or 5 February.

If the person's birthdate occurs between 1 January and 4 February, take the *previous year* as the birth year.

Examples:
(a) *Birthdates before 4 February*
Mr Lee was born on 12 January 1944; therefore to calculate the Natal Number, the year of birth is considered to be 1943.

(b) *Birthdate being 4 February*
Mr Lo was born on 4 February 1948. In 1948, Spring Begins

occurred on 5 February. Consequently, 4 February must have belonged to the previous solar year, and Mr Lo's birth year is adjusted to 1947.

(c) *Birthdate 5 February and later*
Mr Cheng was born on 5 February 1952. There is no need to check the tables to find the date of Spring Begins for 1952, because whether Spring Begins occurred on 4 or 5 February, 5 February would still be a date in the new solar year. Therefore the birth year remains 1952.

The Annual Number for a *man* is the same as the Annual Number for the year he is born; as has been mentioned already, the Annual Numbers progress in reverse order. The Annual Number for a *woman*, however, progresses in direct sequence; the male and female annual numbers coincide at number 3. This is much more clearly understood once the numbers are set out in a table. Here, for example, are the numbers for the solar years from 1985 to 2003.

SOLAR YEAR CORRESPONDING TO	ANNUAL NUMBER	MALE ANNUAL NUMBER	FEMALE ANNUAL NUMBER
1985	6	6	9
1986	5	5	1
1987	4	4	2
1988	3	3	3
1989	2	2	4
1990	1	1	5
1991	9	9	6
1992	8	8	7
1993	7	7	8
1994	6	6	9
1995	5	5	1
1996	4	4	2
1997	3	3	3
1998	2	2	4
1999	1	1	5
2000	9	9	6
2001	8	8	7
2002	7	7	8
2003	6	6	9

From this, it is a simple matter to calculate the Annual Number for any year.

The following formulas enable the Annual Number to be calculated simply without the necessity for tables. Observe, however, that these formulas are only appropriate for years of the twentieth-century.

Formula for calculating the Annual Number for a Man (for a twentieth-century date only):

Formula:
Male Annual Number = 10 − (z modulus 9), where z is the number represented by the last two digits of the solar year.

Method:
   (a) Take the last two digits of the solar year.
   (b) Divide by 9.
   (c) If the remainder is 0, let it be 9.
   (d) Subtract the remainder from 10.

The result is the Male Annual Number.

Formula for calculating the Annual Number for a Woman (for a twentieth-century date only):

Formula:
Female Annual Number = (z + 5) modulus 9, where z is the number represented by the last two digits of the solar year.

Method:
   (a) Take the last two digits of the solar year.
   (b) Add 5.
   (c) Divide the result by 9.
   (d) If the remainder is 0, let it be 9.

The remainder is the Female Annual Number.

Exercises

Example 1. Find the Annual Number for a man born 14 September 1957.

Example 2. Find the Annual Number for a woman born 4 July 1962.

Example 3. Find the Annual Number for a man born 3 January 1955.

Example 4. Find the Annual Number for a woman born 2 February 1959.

Worked Examples

Example 1. Find the Annual Number for a man born 14 September. The date is after 4 February so no adjustment needs to be made to the date.

Take the last two digits of 1957:	57
Divide 57 by 9; note the remainder:	6, remainder 3
Take remainder from 10:	7

Therefore, the Male Annual Number is 7.

Example 2. Find the Annual Number for a woman born 4 July 1962. The date is after 4 February, so no adjustment needs to be made to the date.

Take the last two digits of 1962:	62
Add 5:	67
Divide 67 by 9; note the remainder:	7, remainder 4

Therefore, the Female Annual Number is 4.

Example 3. Find the Annual Number for a man born 3 January 1955. The date is before 4 February, so take previous year: i.e. 1955 becomes 1954.

Take the last two digits of 1954:	54
Divide 54 by 9; note the remainder:	6, remainder 0
Let remainder 0 be 9.	
Take 9 from 10:	1

Therefore, the Male Annual Number is 1.

Example 4. Find the Annual Number for a woman born 2 February 1959. The date is before 4 February, so take previous year: i.e. 1959 becomes 1958.

Take the last two digits of 1958	58
Add 5:	63
Divide 63 by 9; note the remainder:	7, remainder 0
Let remainder 0 be 9.	

Therefore, the Female Annual Number is 9.

To Find the Solar Month and Natal Number

Turn to the table of Natal Numbers that follows. In the first column of the table will be found the approximate date on which the Solar Month begins. In most cases, it will be a simple matter to see which Solar Month the person was born in.

Now examine the right-hand part of the table. Notice first that this part of the table is divided into Male and Female. Look at the head of the relevant Male or Female columns to find the one that is headed by the person's Annual Number, already calculated earlier. By cross referring to the relevant Solar Month, the person's Natal Number, or Feng Shui Horoscope Number, will be found.

Once the Natal Number has been found, we can find which directions are most appropriate for that person and, as a consequence, what parts of a house or workplace would be most conducive to their well-being. To discover this, we must examine the attributes of each of the nine Natal Numbers. Before that, however, the reader should continue the examples given at the end of the previous section, and determine the Natal Numbers for each case.

Exercises

Continue the previous exercises by finding the relevant Natal Numbers.

1. Find the Natal Number for a man born 14 September 1957.
   From the earlier worked example, the Annual Number is known to be 7.
   From the Table of Natal Numbers, 14 September is seen to occur during the ——— Solar Month (beginning 7-9 September). The Annual Number 7 is found at the top of the ——— double-column; we take the ——— column as we are looking for the Natal Number for a man. In this column, alongside the ——— month, is the figure ———. Therefore, the required Natal Number is ———.

2. Find the Natal Number for a woman born 4 July 1962.

3. Find the Natal Number for a man born 3 January 1955.

4. Find the Natal Number for a woman born 2 February 1959.

Worked Examples

1. *Find the Natal Number for a man born 14 September 1957.*

From the earlier worked example, the Annual Number is known to be 7.

From the Table of Natal Numbers, 14 September is seen to occur during the 8th Solar Month (beginning 7-9 September). The Annual Number 7 is found at the top of the first (1 4 7) double-column; we take the left hand (m) part as we are looking for the Natal Number for a man. In this column, alongside the 8th month, is the figure 1. Therefore, the required Natal Number is 1.

2. *Find the Natal Number for a woman born 4 July 1962.*

From the earlier worked example, the Annual Number is known to be 4.

From the Table of Natal Numbers, 4 July is seen to occur during the 5th Solar Month (beginning 5-7 June). The Annual Number 4 is found at the top of the first (1 4 7) double-column; we take the right hand (f) part as we are looking for the Natal Number for a woman. In this column, alongside the 5th Month, is the figure 2. Therefore the required Natal Number is 2.

3. *Find the Natal Number for a man born 3 January 1955.*

From the earlier worked example, the Annual Number is known to be 1.

From the Table of Natal Numbers, 3 January is seen to occur during the 11th Solar Month (beginning 7-8 December). The Annual Number 1 is found at the top of the first (1 4 7) double-column, we take the left hand (m) part as we are looking for the Natal Number for a man. In this column, alongside the 11th month, is the figure 7. Therefore the required Natal Number is 7.

4. *Find the Natal Number for a woman born 2 February 1959.*

From the earlier worked example, the Annual Number is known to be 9.

From the Table of Natal Numbers, 2 February is seen to occur during the 12th Solar Month (beginning 5-7 January). The Annual Number 9 is found at the top of the third (3 6 9) double-column; we take the right hand (f) part as we are looking for the Natal Number for a woman. In this column, alongside the 12th month, is the figure 3. Therefore the required Natal Number is 3.

TABLE OF SOLAR MONTHS AND NATAL NUMBERS						
APPROXIMATE DATE of commencement of SOLAR MONTH	ANNUAL NUMBER					
	1 4 7		2 5 8		3 6 9	
	m	f	m	f	m	f
1st *month beginning* 4-5 Feb	8	7	2	4	5	1
2nd *month beginning* 5-7 Mar	7	8	1	5	4	2
3rd *month beginning* 4-6 Apr	6	9	9	6	3	3
4th *month beginning* 5-7 May	5	1	8	7	2	4
5th *month beginning* 5-7 June	4	2	7	8	1	5
6th *month beginning* 7-8 July	3	3	6	9	9	6
7th *month beginning* 7-9 Aug	2	4	5	1	8	7
8th *month beginning* 7-9 Sept	1	5	4	2	7	8
9th *month beginning* 8-9 Oct	9	6	3	3	6	9
10th *month beginning* 7-8 Nov	8	7	2	4	5	1
11th *month beginning* 7-8 Dec	7	8	1	5	4	2
12th *month beginning* 5-7 Jan	6	9	9	6	3	3

To Find the Attributes of the Nine Natal Numbers

Each of the nine Natal Numbers has several attributes, particularly its trigram, from which we can find its direction, polarity (*yin* or *yang*), weft (or horizontal axis—that is, whether it favours an eastward or westward direction), sign (positive or negative), and, above all, the element. Let us examine these attributes in more detail in turn.

Trigram and Direction

We know that each of the trigrams is associated with one of the outer numbers of the *Lo Shu* (see above, p. 109). Additionally, ancient writings tell us that the number 5, at the centre, is represented by the *Ken*, north-east, trigram for males, and the *K'un*, south-westerly, trigram for females. (*Readers who would like to know the reasoning behind this apparently arbitrary decision may read on. Those less interested in academic technicalities can omit this paragraph.*) The most masculine trigram is *Ch'ien*, at the north-west point, and the most feminine is *K'un*, at the south-west. But the element associated with the number 5 is Earth, and whereas *K'un* is an Earth trigram, *Ch'ien* is Metal, which would be unsuitable. But as *K'un* is the most appropriate trigram for females, the male trigram is taken to be the one opposite *K'un*— *Ken*, at the north-east, which happily is also an 'Earth' trigram.

From the Natal Number and the *Lo Shu*, therefore, we can find the trigram and the direction.

Polarity

Although the polarity (whether it is *yin* or *yang*) of the number is derived from the trigram, there is a much easier way to find it. Simply note whether the Natal Number is odd (*yang*) or even (*yin*); the only exception, of course, is the Natal Number 5, since this does not actually have a trigram of its own. As might be expected, it is *yang* for males, and *yin* for females.

Weft

The *weft* of the trigram reveals whether it inclines towards the east or the west.

Those which incline towards the east are:

1	*K'an*	North
3	*Chen*	East
4	*Sun*	South-east
9	*Li*	South

Note that these include one quarter of the compass, and the two poles, north and south. The remaining four incline towards the west:

2 (5, f)	*K'un*	South-west
6	*Ch'ien*	North-west
7	*Tui*	West
8 (5, m)	*Ken*	North-east

It is useful to know the weft when moving house, or changing one's locality. (See p. 139.)

Bias

The 'sign' of the trigram—that is to say, whether a trigram is 'left' or 'right', as distinct from *yang* or *yin*—depends on whether it belongs to the north-eastern half of the compass dial or to the south western side. It follows that the left trigrams are the direct opposite of the right ones:

	LEFT				RIGHT	
6	*Chi'en*	North-west		4	*Sun*	South-east
1	*K'an*	North		9	*Li*	South
8	*Ken*	North-east		2	*K'un*	South-west
3	*Chen*	East		7	*Tui*	West

In the Summary at the end of this section, you will see that the 'Bias' matches the polarity for the first five Natal Numbers (including masculine 5) and then (from feminine 5) is the opposite for the latter five.

The Element

We have seen in an earlier chapter how the four main compass points and the centre are each associated with one of the Five Elements. These are:

North	Water
East	Wood
Centre	Earth
South	Fire
West	Metal

The remaining four 'corners' are considered to belong to the following elements:

North-east						Earth
South-east						Wood
South-west						Earth
North-west						Metal

SUMMARY TABLE OF THE ATTRIBUTES OF THE NATAL NUMBERS

NATAL NUMBER	TRIGRAM	DIRECTION	POLARITY	WEFT	BIAS	ELEMENT
1	*K'an*	North	*Yang*	East	left	Water
2	*K'un*	South-west	*Yin*	West	right	Earth
3	*Chen*	East	*Yang*	East	left	Wood
4	*Sun*	South-east	*Yin*	East	right	Wood
5 (m)	*Ken*	North-east	*Yang*	West	left	Earth
5 (f)	*K'un*	South-west	*Yin*	West	right	Earth
6	*Ch'ien*	North-west	*Yin*	West	left	Metal
7	*Tui*	West	*Yang*	West	right	Metal
8	*Ken*	North-east	*Yin*	West	left	Earth
9	*Li*	South	*Yang*	East	right	Fire

Not all of these aspects are essential for calculating the Feng Shui Horoscope. The polarity, weft, and bias are technical interpretations of the trigrams and may be ignored. A few remarks on their function, however, are included in the final chapter 'More Advanced Feng Shui' (p. 165) for the sake of completeness.

The Building and its Residents

We have now looked at the various attributes of the Natal Number. What we really want to know is, how does this help us to know which parts of a building are the ones most suitable for a particular person, and which ones ought to be avoided?

In the previous section, we saw that the orientation of a building produces certain portents that mean that certain parts of the building are, *in general*, beneficial or harmful. We are now going to see how the orientation of a building affects each individual, depending on that person's own Natal Number. Later, we shall compare the two findings. First, however, let us see how the Natal Number is matched with the orientation of the building.

The method is based on the sequences of the elements. In effect, the method is no different from the one used to say whether a building was appropriate to its surroundings. However, instead of speaking of, say, a Fire-type house in a Wood environment, we are looking at the way a person relates to the room by comparing the element of the person's Natal Number with the element of the room it is proposed to occupy.

This is the procedure; it should have a familiar ring to it.

Reminder:
The generative order of the elements is WOOD→FIRE→ EARTH→METAL→WATER→(WOOD)
The destructive order of the elements is WOOD→EARTH→ WATER→FIRE→METAL→(WOOD)

Note the element associated with the compass direction of the room of the house (the 'placing').

Note the element of the person's Natal Number.

THEN

If the element of the placing *generates* the element of the Natal Number, the placing is extremely favourable. If the element of the placing *destroys* the element of the Natal Number, then the placing is extremely unfavourable.

If the element of the placing *matches* that of the element of the Natal Number, the situation is favourable.

If the element of the Natal Number *generates* the element of the placing, the situation is weak and inadvisable.

If the element of the Natal Number *destroys* the element of the placing, the situation is mildly favourable.

The above rules can be shown diagrammatically.

A

E   B

D   C

If we suppose that the element of the Natal Number is A, and the other four elements follow in the generative sequence, then:

If the placing is element A, this is favourable;
If the placing is element B, this is weak;
If the placing is element C, this is mildly favourable;
If the placing is element D, this is most favourable;

If the placing is element E, this is very favourable.

Summary of the Method

It follows that in order to find which rooms or areas of a building are most suited to a particular individual, we need to know the following:

The person's Natal Number;
The element associated with the Natal Number;
The situation of the room in respect to the rest of the building (its compass-bearing);
The element associated with this compass bearing.

However, we shall soon see how we can save ourselves some trouble by side-stepping one of these factors. For the moment, however, let us proceed by drawing up a table to show the essential data, thus:

NATAL NUMBER_____

ELEMENT_____

ROOM DIRECTION_____

ROOM ELEMENT_____

Next, we shall write down the Eight Directions, and their associated elements (include the Centre if the building has a central, windowless room):

ELEMENT	FAVOURABILITY	DIRECTION
Water	_____	North
Earth	_____	North-east
Wood	_____	East
Wood	_____	South-east
Fire	_____	South
Earth	_____	South-west
Metal	_____	West
Metal	_____	North-west

Now we refer back to the element of the Natal Number.
Under 'Favourability' we can mark two ticks (very favourable)

against the element that *generates* the element of the Natal Number.

Then we mark one tick (favourable) against the element that is the same as the element of the Natal Number, and one tick against the element that is *destroyed* by the Natal Element.

Conversely, two crosses (very unfavourable) are marked against the element that destroys the Natal Element, and one cross (weak) against the one that is produced by the Natal Element.

We can now see at a glance which directions are going to be beneficial, and which not. This table therefore takes us straight to the answer we want, without having to bother about the element of the orientation of each room.

The reader should have no difficulty in completing similar tables for the four examples above.

Exercises

Complete tables showing which directions are beneficial or otherwise for the four examples above.

1. Indicate which directions are favourable or otherwise for a male client born 14 September 1957.

Method:
From the worked examples, we know the Natal Number to be 1.

From the Table of Attributes, we know the element of Natal Number 1 to be (A).
   Element A is produced by element E: very favourable.
   Element A is favourable with itself.
   Element A produces element B: weak.
   Element A destroys element C: mildly favourable.
   Element A is destroyed by element D: very unfavourable.

Reminder
The generative order of the elements is WOOD→FIRE→EARTH→METAL→WATER→(WOOD)
The destructive order of the elements is WOOD→EARTH→FIRE→METAL→(WOOD)

Complete the table.

2. Indicate which directions are favourable or otherwise for a female client born 4 July 1962.

3. Indicate which directions are favourable or otherwise for a male client born 3 January 1955.

4. Indicate which directions are favourable or otherwise for a female client born 2 February 1959.

Workings

Example 1. From earlier working of the examples, we know the Natal Number for 14 September 1957 to be 1.
From the tables, we know that the element for Natal Number 1 is Water.

Water is produced by Metal: very favourable.	✓✓
Water is favourable with itself.	✓
Water produces Wood: weak.	x
Water destroys Fire: mildly favourable.	✓
Water is destroyed by Earth: very unfavourable.	xx

Example 2. From earlier working of the examples, we know the Natal Number for 4 July 1962 to be 2.
From the tables, we know that the element for Natal Number 2 is Earth.

Earth is produced by Fire: very favourable.	✓✓
Earth is favourable with itself.	✓
Earth produces Metal: weak.	x
Earth destroys Water: mildly favourable.	✓
Earth is destroyed by Wood: very unfavourable.	xx

Example 3. From earlier working of the examples, we know the Natal Number for 3 January 1955 to be 7.
From the tables, we know that the element for Natal Number 7 is Metal.

Metal is produced by Earth: very favourable.	✓✓
Metal is favourable with itself.	✓
Metal produces Water: weak.	x
Metal destroys Wood: mildly favourable.	✓
Metal is destroyed by Fire: very unfavourable.	xx

> *Example 4.* From earlier working of the examples, we know the Natal Number for 2 February 1959 to be 3.
>
> From the tables, we know that the element for Natal Number 3 is Wood.
>
> Wood is produced by Water: very favourable.   ✓✓
>
> Wood is favourable with itself.   ✓
>
> Wood produces Fire: weak.   x
>
> Wood destroys Earth: mildly favourable.   ✓
>
> Wood is destroyed by Metal: very unfavourable.   xx

Comparing the Suitability of Rooms for Different Persons

We can now compile the above observations into a table. If we include all the observations in one table, and compare the results, we can see at a glance that certain rooms favour one person, but not others. This is a useful exercise when assessing the Feng Shui of a shared house, or business premises run by a partnership.

ELEMENT	FAVOURABILITY				DIRECTION
	CLIENT 1	CLIENT 2	CLIENT 3	CLIENT 4	
Water	✓	✓	x	✓✓	North
Earth	xx	✓	✓✓	✓	North-east
Wood	x	xx	✓	✓	East
Wood	x	xx	✓	✓	South-east
Fire	✓	✓✓	xx	x	South
Earth	xx	✓	✓✓	✓	South-west
Metal	✓✓	x	✓	xx	West
Metal	✓✓	x	✓	xx	North-west

Home and Horoscope: The Auspices

If we wish, instead of simply saying that a particular room is favourable or not for a particular person, we can look at the ways that the elements interact and be more precise in our assessment. Here is a brief guide to the way each element of the building's interior relates to the element of the Natal Number.

ROOM ELEMENT: WOOD
Personal Element: Wood
This is a stable and creative atmosphere. It would be suitable for

a study, lounge, or office. If the Natal Number is that of an infant, this would be suitable for a bedroom.

ROOM ELEMENT: WOOD
Personal Element: Fire
An excellent choice for a study or work-room, particularly for a creative person, being very stimulating for intelligence. If the personal element in this case is that of an infant, this room would be an excellent choice for a bedroom, as it would ensure vigorous health and growth.

ROOM ELEMENT: WOOD
Personal Element: Earth
This is not an ideal choice. The client should not spend long periods in this room as it would be found to be debilitating; the client may become easily tired and lack-lustre after a short time.

ROOM ELEMENT: WOOD
Personal Element: Metal
After short periods in this room the client would feel very energetic. A good choice for a workshop, or for recreational activities, perhaps a personal gymnasium. Not, perhaps, such a good choice for a bedroom.

ROOM ELEMENT: WOOD
Personal Element: Water
The effect here is similar to that on people with a personal Earth element; the atmosphere is weakening. It is inadvisable to spend long periods here.

*   *   *

ROOM ELEMENT: FIRE
Personal Element: Wood
A highly inappropriate situation. The person would feel uncomfortable; with regard to health, there would be an inclination to fevers and nervous complaints. Avoid.

ROOM ELEMENT: FIRE
Personal Element: Fire
Not the ideal spot, but harmless. Although it can be stimulating for a short while, long periods spent here may result in restlessness. Ideal for a household accounts office, or a room where short bursts of activity take place from time to time.

ROOM ELEMENT: FIRE
Personal Element: Earth
A very sound environment. This could be the client's main bedroom. This room has a comfortable, encouraging atmosphere.

ROOM ELEMENT: FIRE
Personal Element: Metal
Avoid this room, either for a bedroom (it introduces lethargy and laziness) or for an office (finances fritter away inexplicably).

ROOM ELEMENT: FIRE
Personal Element: Water
There is no harm to be had in spending short periods in this room; nevertheless, the client will feel uncomfortable here, particularly in dealing with other people. Do not use this room for a lounge, for example.

*   *   *

ROOM ELEMENT: EARTH
Personal Element: Wood
This room could be used as a bedroom, or for study or leisure; for a few years it will be found to be comfortable enough, but eventually the client will tire of it and want a change. The feeling of unease may lead the client into thinking that a move to a new location is necessary, but in fact it is merely that the resources of this room have been exhausted.

ROOM ELEMENT: EARTH
Personal Element: Fire
There is a weakening atmosphere to this room. The client should avoid spending long periods here.

ROOM ELEMENT: EARTH
Personal Element: Earth
This is a stable, comfortable room, which the client will enjoy. Excellent for a cosy nook, lounge, or bedroom. If chosen for a study, however, little work would get done. Perhaps the client's favourite room in the house.

ROOM ELEMENT: EARTH
Personal Element: Metal
The ideal location for a study or office. Very stimulating and beneficial for health and finances. If used as a bedroom, the client will wake refreshed every morning.

ROOM ELEMENT: EARTH
Personal Element: Water
Avoid this room. Its weakening effect is felt most strongly on the client's judgement and self-esteem. If this room is used as a bedroom, the client's health and personal behaviour will deteriorate, leading to a loss of friends.

ROOM ELEMENT: METAL
Personal Element: Wood
Avoid this room. It has a deleterious effect. The creative person would lose imaginative drive. If used as a bedroom, there is a risk of ill-health; in other rooms, the danger of physical injury through accident is heightened.

ROOM ELEMENT: METAL
Personal Element: Fire
This room has an easy-going atmosphere, neither harmful nor beneficial. Most probably the client will not even notice this room; it may be a passage or utility room that is taken for granted.

ROOM ELEMENT: METAL
Personal Element: Earth
If the client finds it difficult to manage finances, or if there is a chronic illness that is likely to need surgery, no harm will be done by seeing if the client is spending long periods in a room under the influence of the element Metal. Not advisable for bedroom, office, or lounge.

ROOM ELEMENT: METAL
Personal Element: Metal
Ideal for the home office, or, in business premises, the accounts office. A sound atmosphere for financial matters.

ROOM ELEMENT: METAL
Personal Element: Water
An excellent spot for either the bedroom or the office. In business premises, this will ideally be used for the client's office, especially if there is a need for frequent dealings with other people.

*   *   *

ROOM ELEMENT: WATER
Personal Element: Wood
An excellent choice for the bedroom, the study, or office. If the room is used for any other function, the highly stimulating and beneficial influences of this room are likely to be lost. Harness them to good effect on the health and well-being of the client.

ROOM ELEMENT: WATER
Personal Element: Fire
An unsatisfactory atmosphere. If used for a bedroom, sleep is restless; as an office, the malign influences are manifested in the client's inability to concentrate. Avoid this room.

ROOM ELEMENT: WATER
Personal Element: Earth
This could be a satisfactory environment for a room of secondary importance. Do not use it for the main bedroom, or in business premises for the main office; for a short-term office or recreation room it would be quite suitable.

ROOM ELEMENT: WATER
Personal Element: Metal
There is a weakening atmosphere here; if the room is used for a bedroom, the client would wake tired and unrefreshed; if used as an office or study, there would be an inability to concentrate. As a result, the client may lose his grip on financial affairs. Not recommended.

ROOM ELEMENT: WATER
Personal Element: Water
Quite a satisfactory environment here for a writer's study or the musician's practice room. It might also be thought of as a suitable location for a library. A bedroom here would be quiet and peaceful; a lounge restful.

Comparing the Portents of the Building with the Natal Number

In an earlier section, we saw how the orientation of a building affected the beneficial qualities of each room, according to the direction it faced. Then we saw how the orientation of each room reacted with the personal Feng Shui horoscopes of people in the house.

Now we shall compare the two sets of data and see how each person is affected by the orientation of the building and the direction occupied by each room.

We already have all the information we need. All that is left to do is collate the information into a table.

We proceed exactly as on p. 101, this time writing down the names of the portents for each of the directions and marking the ticks or crosses to show whether the portents are favourable or otherwise.

The 'rating' for favourability should be as follows:

A Six Curses	Not favourable	x
B Five Ghosts	Not favourable	x
C Severed Fate	Very unfavourable	xx
D Lengthened Years	Very favourable	✓✓
E Accident and Mishap	Very unfavourable	xx
F Generating Breath	Very favourable	✓✓
G Celestial Monad	Favourable	✓
H Direction faced	Favourable	✓

As before, the information can be set out in a table.

ORIENTATION OF BUILDING_____

DIRECTION	KEY LETTER AND NAME OF PORTENT		FAVOURABILITY
North	_____	_____	_____
North-east	_____	_____	_____
East	_____	_____	_____
South-east	_____	_____	_____
South	_____	_____	_____
South-west	_____	_____	_____
West	_____	_____	_____
North-west	_____	_____	_____

Now we can compare the overall favourability of each room according to the orientation of the building, with the particular favourability of each room according to the Natal Number of each person residing in the building. For each person note:

Natal Number   _____
Element of Natal Number   _____
Orientation of Building   _____

ELEMENT	FAVOURABILITY	DIRECTION	PORTENT	FAVOURABILITY
Water	_____	North	_____ :	_____
Earth	_____	North-east	_____ :	_____
Wood	_____	East	_____ :	_____
Wood	_____	South-east	_____ :	_____
Fire	_____	South	_____ :	_____
Earth	_____	South-west	_____ :	_____
Metal	_____	West	_____ :	_____
Metal	_____	North-west	_____ :	_____

It is a simple matter to extend this table to include two or more persons, and so find which rooms are most beneficial for each person, taking into account both the Natal Number of each person in turn and the orientation of the building as a whole.

Here is an example of such a table:

ELEMENT	FAVOURABILITY		DIRECTION	PORTENT	FAVOURABILITY
	(1)	(2)			
Water	____ :	____	North	_____ :	_____
Earth	____ :	____	North-east	_____ :	_____
Wood	____ :	____	East	_____ :	_____
Wood	____ :	____	South-east	_____ :	_____
Fire	____ :	____	South	_____ :	_____
Earth	____ :	____	South-west	_____ :	_____
Metal	____ :	____	West	_____ :	_____
Metal	____ :	____	North-west	_____ :	_____

The best way to see how this table functions is to take an example.

Suppose, for instance, that the two men in our previous examples have set up business together and have bought premises into which they are about to move. Readers may like to tackle the exercise for themselves first, or follow through the working.

Once the table is completed, of course, the most important thing is to summarize your findings and advise on the suitability of each room for various purposes.

Case Studies

Case 1

Two men have bought business premises for a joint partnership. Advise on the allocation of space.

Their birthdates are (A) 14 September 1957 and (B) 3 January 1955.

The premises face North-east.

Case 2

Two sisters have bought a house. Advise on the allocation of bedrooms.

Their birthdates are (A) 4 July 1962 and (B) 2 February 1959. The house faces West.

Working Method

From the birthdate, find the Natal Number.

From the Natal Number, find the personal element.

Note the orientation of the building.

This information should be transferred to the heading of the table, shown below.

We turn to the table below, and alongside each element (note that certain elements appear twice in the table) we mark ticks or crosses according to whether the element of the room is favourable with the personal element, or otherwise.

Next we take the orientation of the building. We find the appropriate chart on p. 101, then jot down the key letters of the portents—at this stage there is no need to write down their actual names—alongside the relevant compass directions. The next stage is to mark ticks or crosses in the table according to whether the portents are favourable or otherwise.

Finally, the ticks and crosses for the Natal Number should be added to the ticks and crosses for the room's orientation.

The rooms pertaining to those directions that have most ticks are obviously more suitable for that particular person than rooms with fewer ticks, or with crosses.

Instead, however, of leaving the matter at that, the careful Feng Shui consultant should, by noting the remarks on the portents on pp. 102-3, and the remarks regarding the interaction of elements on p. 126ff, make a few pertinent suggestions relevant to the client's case.

Case 1

Two men have bought business premises for a joint partnership. Advise

on the allocation of space. Their birthdates are (A) 14 September 1957 and (B) 3 January 1955. The premises face North-east.

Birthdate (A): 14 September 1957
Birthdate (B): 3 January 1955
Orientation of building: North-east

From previous worked examples we know the Natal Number and Element for the two men, and have already compiled a table of favourability (see p. 125). We complete the heading of the table below, and copy our previous findings into the appropriate spaces.

We then note the orientation of the building, and turn to the charts on p. 101. From these charts, we see that for a North-east type of building, the following portents apply for each direction:

Direction		Portent	Favourability	
North	G	Celestial Monad	Favourable	✓
North-east	H	Direction faced	Favourable	✓
East	A	Six Curses	Not favourable	x
South-east	B	Five Ghosts	Not favourable	x
South	C	Severed Fate	Very Unfavourable	xx
South-west	D	Lengthened Years	Very Favourable	✓✓
West	E	Accident and Mishap	Very Unfavourable	xx
North-west	F	Generating Breath	Very Favourable	✓✓

Client A: Natal Number......1
         Personal Element......Water
Client B: Natal Number 7
         Personal Element......Metal
Orientation of Building ......North-east

ELEMENT	FAVOURABILITY		DIRECTION	PORTENT		FAVOURABILITY
	(A)	(B)				
Water	✓	x	North	G	:	✓
Earth	xx	✓✓	North-east	H	:	✓
Wood	x	✓	East	A	:	x
Wood	x	✓	South-east	B	:	x
Fire	✓	xx	South	C	:	xx
Earth	xx	✓✓	South-west	D	:	✓✓
Metal	✓✓	✓	West	E	:	xx
Metal	✓✓	✓	North-west	F	:	✓✓

Now we summarize the above table:

	Client A	Client B
North:	✓ ✓	x ✓

Suitable for Client A; less so for Client B.

North-east: x x ✓ / ✓ ✓ ✓
Unsuitable for Client A; very suitable for Client B.

East x x / ✓ x
Unsuitable for Client A; fair for Client B.

South-east: x x / ✓ x
Unsuitable for Client A; fair for Client B.

South: ✓ x x / x x x x
Not suitable for Client A; disastrous for Client B.

South-west: x x ✓ ✓ / ✓ ✓ ✓ ✓
Fairly suitable for Client A; excellent for Client B.

West: ✓ ✓ x x / ✓ x x
Fairly suitable for Client A; less so for Client B.

North-west: ✓ ✓ ✓ ✓ / ✓ ✓ ✓
Excellent for Client A; very good for Client B.

From this summary, we can see that the North-west location is excellent for Client A, and very good for Client B; the portents are 'Generating Breath'. This should be the power centre of the organization, with Client A having his office here. Client B's best situation is farther away, in the South-west. There could be an intervening dead space, such as a cloakroom, between the two offices. The South position does not favour either client, so this area would be best used for storage.

Case 2

Two sisters have bought a house. Advise on the allocation of bedrooms. Their birthdates are (A) 4 July 1962 and (B) 2 February 1959. The house faces West.

From previous worked examples we know the Natal Number and Element for the two sisters, and have already compiled a table of favourability (see p. 124). Following the working of the example above, a table is compiled.

Client A: Natal Number......2
        Personal Element......Earth
Client B: Natal Number......3
        Personal Element......Wood
Orientation of Building ......West

ELEMENT	FAVOURABILITY (A)	(B)	DIRECTION	PORTENT	FAVOURABILITY
Water	√	√√	North	E	xx
Earth	√	√	North-east	D	√√
Wood	xx	√	East	C	xx
Wood	xx	√	South-east	A	x
Fire	√√	x	South	B	x
Earth	√	√	South-west	G	√
Metal	x	xx	West	H	√
Metal	x	xx	North-west	F	√√

Summarizing the above table:

	Client A	**Client B**
North:	√ x x	√ √ x x

    Unsuitable for Client A; fair for Client B.

| North-east: | √ √ √ | √ √ √ |

    Highly suitable for both clients

| East | x x x x | √ x x |

    Disastrous for Client A; unsuitable for Client B.

| South-east: | x x x | √ x |

    Unsuitable for Client A; fair for Client B.

| South: | √ √ x | x x |

    Fairly suitable for Client A; unsuitable for Client B.

| South-west: | √ √ | √ √ |

    Good for both clients.

| West: | x √ | x x √ |

    Fair for Client A; poor for Client B.

| North-west: | x √ √ | x x √ √ |

    Quite good for Client A; fair for Client B.

Unfortunately, the ladies have not chosen the ideal orientation for their house. There are a couple of locations that are ideally suited to both; these rooms should be ones they might use jointly, such as the dining-room, or the living-room. On the other hand, there are no other rooms that might be suitable for either of the sisters' own rooms; consequently, it might be that the 'three-tick' rooms in the North-east should be allocated to one of the sisters and the 'two-tick' room at the opposite end of the house to the other. If we look back at the table of family relationships on p. 95, we see that neither of these trigrams represents sisterly relationships, although *Ken* (North-east) represents the younger son, and *K'un* (South-west) the Mother. Possibly, therefore, the elder sister should take the South-west room. Unfortunately, because of the orientation of the house that the sisters have chosen, there are no really good Feng Shui places; the beneficial aspects of their personal elements are cancelled out by the inauspicious influences of the orientation of the house.

In a case like this, the geomancer might suggest that, if there was a side entrance, this might be construed as the main door by making some alteration to the interior layout of the house or by diverting the approach path. It really would depend on what the ladies were prepared to do in order to improve the Feng Shui of their house.

In the next chapter, we shall take a look at the kind of practical advice a geomancer might give clients during a tour of inspection of a business or residential premises.

Further Aspects of the Natal Number

Here are a few more notes on how these aspects of the natal trigrams can be taken into account on such diverse topics as which direction to travel when moving house or which side of the bed a married couple should sleep.

Positioning Two People

Two people sharing a bedroom, or two partners working at benches or desks next to each other, should position themselves so that their natal trigrams integrate.

The rule is:

If the trigrams of two people are of different weft, then:

East-weft should be to the direction which is left-bias of West-weft.

West-weft should be to the direction which is right-bias of East-weft.

If they are of the same weft, the positioning is immaterial. These rules sound complex, but in effect they can be reduced very simply. East-weft trigrams belong to the Natal Numbers 1, 3, 4, and 9; West-weft trigams are the others. So:

Those people whose Natal Numbers are 1, 3, 4, or 9, should position themselves to the East, North-east, North, or North-west of those whose Natal Numbers are 2, 5, 6, 7, or 8, and vice versa.

Travelling and Moving House

Many businessmen in the East consult Feng Shui charts before commencing a journey. Similarly, if it becomes necessary to leave one's native town, to set up home in a different city, or there is an urge to emigrate and start life anew, the Natal Number can advise on the best direction in which to travel.

The rule is:

East-weft has a left-bias;

West-weft has a right-bias.

If the person is obliged to travel in a direction which is contrary to the bias, the journey should be deflected so that the final part of the journey proceeds according to the correct bias.

NW 6	N 1	NE 8,5(m)
W 7		E 3
SW 2,5(f)	S 9	SE 4

Diagram summarizing the Natal Numbers, directions, weft, and bias

Weft

Natal numbers 1, 3, 4, 9, are East weft and are biased towards the 'left' directions.

Natal numbers 2, 5, 6, 7, 8, are West weft and are biased towards the 'right' directions.

Bias
Left bias directions are NW, N, NE, E
Right bias directions are W, SW, S, SE

Completing Your Own Feng Shui Chart

Now that all the steps for constructing a Feng Shui horoscope have been covered, no doubt you will want to compile a chart either for yourself or your friends.

At the end of this section you will find a blank chart for you to complete. To save you searching back through the pages of this book, here is an outline of all the main points, together with the necessary tables. No details are explained here, as these have already been covered in the relevant sections.

Note that the Personal Chart includes space for two persons living in the same residence; this makes it possible to compare the two charts and see whether particular rooms favour one resident more than the other.

Procedure

1. Information required: (Name); birthdate of resident; sex of resident; orientation of building.
   Enter on to Personal Chart.

2. Correct the birth year if birth date is before 4 or 5 February.

3. Calculate Annual Number:

   Male: Take last two digits of corrected solar year
           Divide by 9
           If remainder is 0, call it 9
           Subtract remainder from 10
           Answer is Annual Number

   Female: Take last two digits of corrected solar year
           Add 5
           Divide by 9

If remainder is 0, call it 9
Remainder is Annual Number

4. Find Natal Number from Table A.
   Enter on the Personal Chart.

5. Find the Personal Element from Table B.
   Enter on the Personal Chart.

6. Enter favourability of the elements on the Personal Chart. The
   element which is: Generating: ✓✓
                      Same: ✓
                      Generated: x
                      Destroyed: ✓
                      Destroying: xx

The generative order of the elements is WOOD→FIRE→
EARTH→METAL→WATER→(WOOD)
The destructive order of the elements is WOOD→EARTH→
WATER→FIRE→METAL→(WOOD)

---

7. Find the chart pertaining to the orientation on the Charts of
   Portents.
      Enter the key letters at the appropriate directions on the
   Personal Chart.

8. Note the names of the Portents, and the favourability, from
   Table C.

9. Summarize the favourability of each direction.

10. Comment.

TABLE A TABLE OF SOLAR MONTHS AND NATAL NUMBERS						
APPROXIMATE DATE of commencement of SOLAR MONTH	ANNUAL NUMBER					
	1 4 7		2 5 8		3 6 9	
	m	**f**	**m**	**f**	**m**	**f**
1st *month beginning* 4-5 Feb	8	7	2	4	5	1
2nd *month beginning* 5-7 March	7	8	1	5	4	2
3rd *month beginning* 4-6 April	6	9	9	6	3	3
4th *month beginning* 5-7 May	5	1	8	7	2	4
5th *month beginning* 5-7 June	4	2	7	8	1	5
6th *month beginning* 7-8 July	3	3	6	9	9	6
7th *month beginning* 7-9 August	2	4	5	1	8	7
8th *month beginning* 7-9 Sept	1	5	4	2	7	8
9th *month beginning* 8-9 Oct	9	6	3	3	6	9
10th *month beginning* 7-8 Nov	8	7	2	4	5	1
11th *month beginning* 7-8 Dec	7	8	1	5	4	2
12th *month beginning* 5-7 Jan	6	9	9	6	3	3

TABLE B PERSONAL ELEMENT	
NATAL NUMBER	PERSONAL ELEMENT
1	Water
2	Earth
3	Wood
4	Wood
5 **m**	Earth
5 **f**	Earth
6	Metal
7	Metal
8	Earth
9	Fire

CHART OF PORTENTS

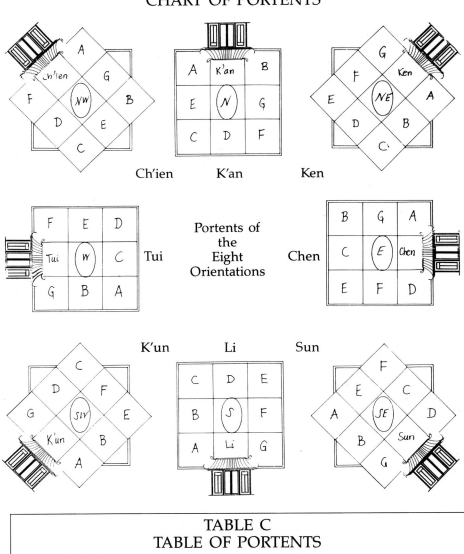

Ch'ien K'an Ken

Tui

Portents of
the
Eight
Orientations

Chen

K'un Li Sun

	TABLE C		
	TABLE OF PORTENTS		
A	Six Curses	Not favourable	x
B	Five Ghosts	Not favourable	x
C	Severed Fate	Very unfavourable	xx
D	Lengthened Years	Very favourable	✓✓
E	Accident and Mishap	Very unfavourable	xx
F	Generating Breath	Very favourable	✓✓
G	Celestial Monad	Favourable	✓
H	Direction faced	Favourable	✓

PERSONAL CHART

First Resident:

Name _____

Birthdate _____

Sex: M/F

Orientation of Building _____

Natal Number _____

Natal Element_____

Second Resident:

Name _____

Birthdate _____

Sex: M/F

Orientation of Building _____

Natal Number _____

Natal Element_____

ELEMENT	FAVOURABILITY		DIRECTION	PORTENT		FAVOURABILITY
	1st	2nd				
Water	_____	_____	North	_____ :	_____	_____
Earth	_____	_____	North-east	_____ :	_____	_____
Wood	_____	_____	East	_____ :	_____	_____
Wood	_____	_____	South-east	_____ :	_____	_____
Fire	_____	_____	South	_____ :	_____	_____
Earth	_____	_____	South-west	_____ :	_____	_____
Metal	_____	_____	West	_____ :	_____	_____
Metal	_____	_____	North-west	_____ :	_____	_____

PERSONAL CHART

First Resident:

Name _____

Birthdate _____

Sex: M/F

Orientation of Building _____

Natal Number _____

Natal Element_____

Second Resident:

Name _____

Birthdate _____

Sex: M/F

Orientation of Building _____

Natal Number _____

Natal Element_____

ELEMENT	FAVOURABILITY		DIRECTION	PORTENT		FAVOURABILITY
	1st	2nd				
Water	____	____	North	_____ : ____		____
Earth	____	____	North-east	_____ : ____		____
Wood	____	____	East	_____ : ____		____
Wood	____	____	South-east	_____ : ____		____
Fire	____	____	South	_____ : ____		____
Earth	____	____	South-west	_____ : ____		____
Metal	____	____	West	_____ : ____		____
Metal	____	____	North-west	_____ : ____		____

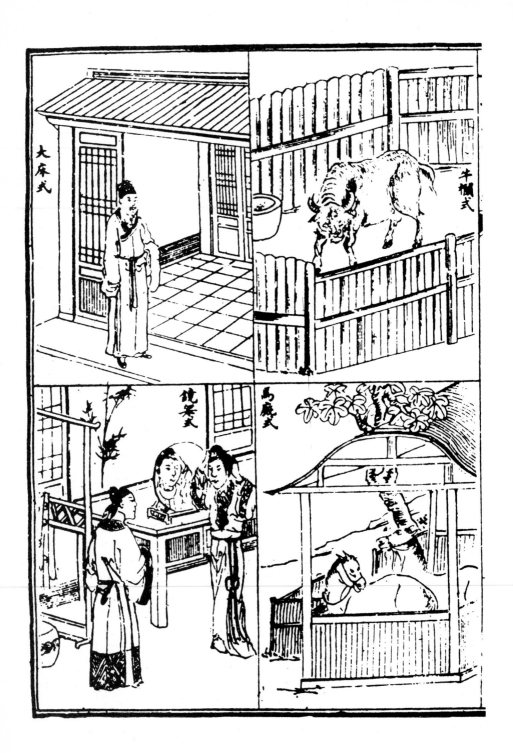

7

Advice and Adages

At the beginning of this book, it was said that there are two main schools of Feng Shui, the Form School and the Compass School, and in the foregoing chapters we have been introduced to the methods used by the practitioners of both of these schools of thought. There is, however, what might be called a third school of Feng Shui that is really a large corpus of dos and don'ts—a heterogeneous assembly of adages drawn from many different sources. Some are half-learned truths from either the Form or Compass schools, some have a kind of logicality behind them, though many of them owe their origins perhaps to ancient shamanism. Thus it is that books on Feng Shui often end with a chapter on talismans and magic writing to ward off the evil spirits of sickness. Quite obviously, such spells have nothing at all to do with either the Form School or Compass School of Feng Shui, yet the Chinese layman happily accepts these adjuncts as an authentic part of the geomancer's profession. Indeed, the client might feel disappointed if the Feng Shui consultant did not leave behind some sealed envelope of secret charms to be buried in the garden, attached to a lintel, or hidden under a carpet. Visitors to China, and those who meet with members of the Chinese communities outside their homeland, will undoubtedly encounter other strange solutions employed to rectify a potentially dangerous Feng Shui situation. The use of cheap bamboo flutes, faceted crystal pendants, tinkly trinkets, and other bric-à-brac is a latter-day response to counter all kinds of ominous Feng Shui circumstances. They are mentioned here for the sake of completeness, but it should be remembered that these folksy remedies are not part of the great traditions of Feng Shui, as carefully expounded by the founders of the Form and Compass Schools, but unorthodox and fanciful additions to what is a sophisticated and precise science.

To this chapter therefore, is added a kind of *omnium gatherum* of popular Feng Shui lore. Many of the solutions offered to combat adverse Feng Shui conditions—for example—the placing of mirrors in strategic places— are based on the principle that malignant currents, *sha*, can be deflected owing to their propensity for straight lines. Other remedies, such as the ubiquitous goldfish bowl, are drawn loosely from the doctrine of the Five Elements. Much of the common repertoire, however, particularly the inevitable use of the symbols of the Eight Trigrams as a universal demonifuge, is not properly part of the authentic canon of Chinese geomancy, although it has become inextricably linked with it.

Correcting Poor Feng Shui Conditions

There are two main classes of remedies when the Feng Shui conditions are potentially harmful.

(a) Those that encourage the flow of *ch'i*, and deflect harmful *sha*.

(b) Those that restore an imbalance of the Five Elements.

To these two categories can be added the talismans, good luck charms, and other baubles that are often posted up to ward off evil spirits or attract good fortune.

The object, when trying to remedy the flow of *ch'i*, is to ensure that they flow around the building unimpeded, ensuring that the favourable currents enter by the main entrance and leave by the rear entrance or a window, ideally passing through each room of the building.

To begin with, the geomancer will usually make suggestions regarding the structure and interior fabric of the building itself. Can a door be re-hung to open in a different direction? Can a wall be built here? Can another entrance or window be placed at this point?

If the householder's finances are not able to run to such lengths, the geomancer then offers less demanding suggestions, such as the placing of mirrors or screens, which might channel the flow of *ch'i* along an alternative route. Mirrors and fans figure prominently in this type of Feng Shui remedy.

The astute Feng Shui consultant, however, will already have assessed the financial limitations of the client before making any proposals, lest the cheaper alternative might be thought to be less effective; the geomancer should leave the client feeling assured, rather than uneasy.

The suggestions offered for rectifying an elemental imbalance can also range from one extreme to the other. If the client is already preparing to make structural changes the geomancer may decide that this would be an ideal opportunity for changing pointed windows (symbolic of Fire) to arched ones (representing Metal) if the surrounding buildings were predominantly rectangular (representing Earth), since Earth generates Metal but is produced by Fire. On the other hand, where such large-scale changes are unlikely to be contemplated, the consultant may simply suggest that some item, symbolic of the controlling element, be introduced into the environment. Plants, water, and colour changes belong to this class of remedy.

Finally, the Chinese Feng Shui adviser may give the client some token such as an envelope containing magical calligraphy, or may suggest that a picture or statuette of a cherished saint or immortal be obtained and positioned at a suitable place for further protection against supernatural agencies.

Encouraging Beneficial *Ch'i*

To find whether beneficial *ch'i* can flow satisfactorily through a building, draw a plan of each floor. It should be possible to draw a line on the plan that begins at the main entrance (or, in the case of an upper floor, from the staircase) and proceeds right through the building, visiting every room on that floor, eventually leaving through a different exit. The *ch'i* should not be expected to leave by the same way they came in; they may, however, branch off into different rooms and leave by a number of exits, like the current of a river that may flow round a number of islets in its course. The flow of *ch'i* through a house can be encouraged by ensuring that all doors open in the direction of the flow.

Entrance doors should, from a Feng Shui point of view, open inwards, despite the fact that in public buildings regulations often stipulate that they should open outwards. House doors invariably open inwards, however, so there is rarely a problem. For public buildings of any kind, a rotating door serves many useful functions: not only does it combine the Feng Shui desirability of an inward entrance with that of the safely stipulation for an outward one, it also allows the *ch'i* to enter and leave by the same way.

If the building has a set of double doors—perhaps the house has a porch, or the office building an entrance hall—both doors or sets of doors should open the same way. If they open in different directions, or are not aligned properly, *ch'i* are prevented from entering the building.

Dead Areas

Areas where the current is unable to flow are dead. Avoid dead corners by filling them with cabinets, large indoor plants, or ornaments.

In locked windowless rooms the *ch'i* perishes and stale *ch'i* have a debilitating effect on those who are obliged to work or sleep near them. Such dead areas only function satisfactorily as storerooms and cupboards. To disperse the dead *ch'i*, ensure that the doors open outwards. There are two important offshoots of this simple observation: garages and assembly rooms.

Modern Feng Shui consultants aver that it is harmful to have a bedroom over a garage, which is a closed space, and therefore one that accumulates dead *ch'i*. The more prosaic reasoning is that fumes from the garage permeate upwards and can act as a slow poison on the sleeper.

Places of entertainment such as cinemas, theatres, and concert halls, which because of their function need to be completely enclosed and windowless, are particularly bad for *ch'i*. Fortunately, for those people who spend only a few hours a week in the environment of dead *ch'i*, the circumstances need not cause undue anxiety. Also, fire regulations usually stipulate that all the doors to such establishments should open outwards, so ensuring the dispersal of dead *ch'i*. But those in charge of rooms used for meetings and other communal purposes, which through some legal loophole escape regular safety inspection, should give urgent consideration to the fact that doors ought to open outwards.

Lost *Ch'i*

Avoid windows at opposite ends of the room. They encourage energizing *ch'i* to flow directly through a room before they have had a chance to stimulate the area with life-enhancing forces. Then, psychologically, a room with windows at opposite ends has no focal point, and it is difficult for anyone in the room to sit—at least mentally—in a comfortable spot. To counteract this, make one window the 'view' and shade the other window in some way. The *ch'i* are encourage to flow round the room before leaving by the 'viewing' window, and the room then possesses a focus.

Similarly, in a house that is divided by a corridor, or one where the rear door is visible from the front entrance, the *ch'i* may flow right through the building without having been prompted to diffuse their beneficial influences. In this case, consideration should be given to the possibility of re-siting the rear entrance. Of course, it is usually impractical to do this, in which case, a favoured solution is to add a porch or even a conservatory to the rear door, to which entrance is gained by the side, rather than in a direction directly opposite to the main entrance.

A simpler solution is to screen the rear entrance from the front by adding a partition or curtain at a convenient place in the passageway, so that the rear entrance is not visible from the front.

The same solutions apply in the case when the stairs greet the front door. It is usually out of the question to consider repositioning the stairwell, though it is not unheard of. Sometimes it is possible to arrange for the foot of the stairs to turn. More practical is the placing of a hall stand or a curtain in front of the stairs, which screens the staircase from the front door.

A common remedy is to install the image of a guardian—like the gargoyles on churches—to ward off baleful influences. The guardian may be a religious picture, the representation of a Taoist deity or saint, a figure of the Buddha, or some watchful animal such as a lion, dog, or dragon. Mirrors, the sign of the Eight Trigrams, wind-chimes, and gongs are all used to the same purpose.

Deflecting Adverse *Sha*

Mirrors

Mirrors are the commonest means used both to encourage the flow of *ch'i* and also to deflect the path of *sha*.

They should be placed at points where the *ch'i* would otherwise come to a dead end, so as to help them on their way. Mirrors are also used to deflect the hidden arrows resulting from sharp angles of buildings pointing at a room. Strategically placed, a *sha*-countering mirror will reflect the threatening image back upon itself, but within the room itself will reveal some other more propitious scene, perhaps a feature of the garden, or water.

But there is an important difference in the placing of those mirrors intended to encourage the flow of *ch'i* and those meant to deflect *sha*. The former should be angled, so that the path of the *ch'i* is bent and sent farther on its way. Mirrors placed to deflect *sha* should reflect them back out of the building.

Mirrors may be used in bathrooms or lavatories where these are enclosed and windowless. The area would otherwise be dead and stagnant. Chinese Feng Shui writers actually report that the people whose toilets are thus 'dead' put their health in danger— the bowels, of course, being the first organ to be affected.

It is important, however, to avoid the careless placing of mirrors in bedrooms. Too stimulating an atmosphere in the bedroom robs the sleeper of rest. Furthermore, there is a Chinese belief that the soul rises at night to leave the body to repose. If, however, the soul catches sight of its own reflection when rising from the body it takes fright and stays to disturb the sleeper's rest with anxious dreams and nightmares.

Instead if it is thought necessary to have a mirror in the room— over a dressing table, perhaps—position it so that it does not reflect the sleeper, but instead enables the door to be seen from the bed. This has the practical advantage of allowing the person in bed to notice if an intruder is at the door.

Beams

On the subjet of bedrooms, the 'third' school of Feng Shui regards it as inauspicious to have beams over the head of the sleeper. If the room is small, and an overhead beam is unavoidable, let it run the length of the bed rather than across it. If it is impossible to have the beam other than going over the bed, then let the bed be positioned so that the beam goes over the body rather than across the head. Perhaps this derives from cases when houses were not as sturdily constructed as might be hoped; if the building collapsed, the beam would do less damage.

Similarly, in a living-room with overhead beams, seating should be so arranged that there are no beams directly over the chairs.

Bridges

Bridges are a particular cause of *sha*. The structure of a bridge is much more substantial than the path or road that leads up to it, and so has been regarded as a potentially dangerous means of funnelling adverse *sha*.

A common means to avert the threat was to erect a stone slab, facing the bridge, on which was carved the motto: '*Shih Kan Tang*', meaning 'The Stone Dares to Resist'. They may also be ornamented with Tigers' heads, or the name of the sacred T'ai Shan mountain.

Shih Kan Tang: Sha-averting stone

Rectifying an Imbalance of Elements

In an earlier section (p. 79) we saw that if there was a potential danger from two elements being unbalanced, the effect could be averted or weakened by introducing a third 'controlling' element at a suitable point. The same rule applies when there is a menacing external feature that can be shown to belong to a particular element type.

When there is only one threatening element, the new element

to be introduced should be one that destroys the threatening element. Alternatively, two elements may be introduced, one of which produces the threatened element, the other of which is threatened by it. When the threat is caused by an 'imbalance' of elements, the element to be introduced should be the 'controlling' element.

Examples of Threatening Elemental Features

The commonest examples of features that threaten sites are:

Wood-type

Columns and pillars, such as lamp-posts and telegraph poles, or even south-sited trees, outside the window. Their shape belongs to the 'Wood' type. Destroying element: Metal.

(This is a very common type of Feng Shui threat, and one which traditionally is countered by the omnipresent goldfish in a bowl. Water is the element that generates Wood, so apparently increasing the threat; but the goldfish, representing Fire, is generated by Wood. Thus the three elements are balanced. This is an example of a compound element remedy.)

Fire-type

Pointed roofs and spires of churches. Destroying element: Water. Introduce a fountain, tap, or drinks dispenser opposite the window. The compound elements are Wood (generating Fire) and Earth (generated by Fire), which is easily effected by placing a living plant standing in soil at a relevant position.

Earth-type

A building whose flat roof is halfway up the view from the window, a church with a tower (temples and churches are disliked—they dispel demons who then have to find another home!), and other disliked features forming a horizontal line produce *sha* of the Earth-type. Wood is the destroying element. The compound element remedy is represented by Fire and Metal, such as candles in a metal bracket.

Metal-type

Metal threats are uncommon but may be seen in the curved roof of a metal gas-holder, or some unusual feature such as ornamental swords or axes on the facades of a temple opposite. The single element remedy is Fire, which might be represented by a hearth fire, candles, or incense; the two-element remedy is Earth and Water, suggesting a water garden of stones and water.

Water-type

Nowadays, Water-type threats may come from electrical installations as well as from the inauspicious configurations of Water patterns we shall meet in the next section. The single-element remedy is Earth, represented by large stone or ceramic ornaments installed at a convenient spot. The two-element remedy—Metal and Wood —can be represented by a number of objects made from these two materials, e.g. an arrangement of dried (not plastic) flowers in a bronze pot.

Now we shall look at the converse of these 'compound-element remedies' and examine some suggestions for ways of redressing an imbalance when the element of the surroundings contrasts with the element at the site.

It may be that the surrounding buildings do not match the element type of the building occupied by the client; or, on a smaller scale, it may be that the element of the trigram of the room's direction contrasts with that of the client's own Natal Trigram.

Here are the ten possible situations, together with suggestions for introducing the controlling element.

Controlling Element to be Wood

When Fire is under threat from Water
or
Water is under threat from Earth.

Wood is represented by columnar shapes, the colour green, and plant life. Depending on the situation, the Feng Shui counsellor might advise on the introduction of indoor plants at a suitable position, a wooden screen or carving (perhaps a Buddha figure, or some Taoist deity), green decoration, or the planting of tall evergreen trees behind the building (never in front).

Controlling Element to be Fire

When Earth is under threat from Wood
or
Wood is under threat from Metal.

Fire is represented by the colour red and sharp angles, as well as by Fire itself. It may be that the actual interior layout of the premises might be redesigned so that the core of the heating system was relocated at an essential spot; a less extreme solution would be the introduction of a splash of fiery red colour, either in the decoration or in soft furnishings.

Controlling Element to be Earth

When Metal is under threat from Fire
or
Fire is under threat from Water.

When the controlling element is to be Earth, the Feng Shui adviser may suggest the creation of a sand garden, the building of an ornamental wall, or, on a smaller scale, the placing of an ornamental ceramic in a carefully designated position. Ochre yellow decorations are another way of representing the Earth element.

Controlling Element to be Metal

When Water is under threat from Earth
or
Earth is under threat from Wood.

Wrought iron railings and metal sculptures are a means of introducing the Metal element. In most cases, however, it may be simpler to rearrange the functions of the interior of a building. In a kitchen, for example, it might be simplest to move the storage of metal utensils to a different position. On a bigger scale, in commercial premises, painting the walls white (the symbolic colour of Metal) could be more appropriate.

Controlling Element to be Water

When Wood is under threat from Metal
or
Metal is under threat from Fire.

When it is impractical to introduce ornamental fountains and water gardens into a building (although these are always extremely popular in the Far East for both their aesthetic and Feng Shui properties) consideration might be given to the provision of handwashing facilities, or chilled water dispensers at the crucial point. Of course, if there is a threat of fire, urgent consideration should be given to the generous provision of fire extinguishers wherever the baleful influence of the Fire element is most marked.

Exercise

Much of this chapter has been almost exclusively of a practical nature, the theoretical side being mostly a revision of previous principles.

The armchair geomancer, however, is invited to browse through the following list, noting which elements are suggested by each item. The exercise is basically an extension of an exercise earlier in this book; here, however, more than one element comes into play.

Aquatic plants
Axe with wooden handle
Black and white unframed abstract painting
Bonsai tree in bowl
Bright red flowers
Bucket of sand
Cactus garden
Carved bamboo pipe, lacquered black
Dried plants in a stone jar
Electric stove
Fountain playing over stones
Gold or brass ornaments
Green painted steel filing cabinet
Incense burning

Pottery oil lamp
Pyramidal glass jar
Red porcelain vase
Sculpture of naturally weatherworn rocks
Silver candelabra
Spherical glass water-dispenser
Water being boiled in a cauldron over a wood fire

Answers

Aquatic plants: Wood, Water
Axe with wooden handle: Wood, Metal
Black and white unframed abstract painting: Metal, Water
Bonsai tree in bowl: Wood, Earth
Bright red flowers: Wood, Fire
Bucket of sand: Earth, Metal
Cactus garden: Earth, Wood
Carved bamboo pipe, lacquered black: Wood, Water
Dried plants in a stone jar: Wood, Earth
Electric stove: Fire, Metal
Fountain playing over stones: Earth, Water
Gold or brass ornaments: Earth, Metal (*Yellow being the colour
   of the Earth element*)
Green painted steel filing cabinet: Wood, Metal
Incense burning: Wood, Fire
Pottery oil lamp: Fire, Earth
Pyramidal glass jar: Fire, Water
Red porcelain vase: Fire, Metal
Sculpture of naturally weatherworn rocks: Earth, Water
Silver candelabra: Fire, Metal
Spherical glass water-dispenser: Metal, Water
Water being boiled in a cauldron over a wood fire: All five
   elements. (*The ash from the fire represents the Earth element*).

The Water Dragon

An important offshoot of the Form School of Feng Shui is the
study of Water Patterns. The Form School, after all, had been deve-
loped in a part of southern China that has always been famous—
even in ancient times—for its spectacular landscape. The Water
Pattern School was introduced by Feng Shui consultants living

in areas that were mainly flat, and thus had few hills or mountains where the terrestrial dragons could be discerned. In these flat marshy places, however, rivers meandered through fantastically twisted waterways, making patterns that could reveal as much to the geomancer as the skyscape of more mountainous regions. Thus, if there were no hills and mountains where the Dragon could be seen, perhaps it could be found in the tortuous windings of river, lake, or spring.

The great philosopher of the Ming dynasty, Chiang Ping-chieh, categorized hundreds of different shapes of water patterns in his book *The Water Dragon Classic,* showing the best sites for buildings that are near water. In fact, the logic behind the reasoning for whether a particular pattern is a good site or otherwise can be reduced to a few basic rules: most of the illustrations in the *Water Dragon Classic* are really extended examples of variations upon these few rules, even though few of the examples would ever be encountered in practice, outside, perhaps, a great commercial dockside, or the canal-founded cities of Venice or Amsterdam.

Basic Water Dragon Principles

(a) It is good for there to be a stretch of water in front of the house. A small pond constructed specially for this purpose is called the *Ming T'ang.* It serves to ensure there is a flat, open stretch in front of the house, in accordance with the rules of Feng Shui (see 'The Ideal Setting' on p. 28).

(a) The *Ming T'ang* (highly favourable)

(b) Water flowing at an angle towards the site brings wealth to those who dwell there. (*Water often symbolizes money.*)

(c) But the water should not flow in a straight line directly towards the site, as it then becomes a carrier of *sha*. (*The inherent dangers of a river flowing directly at the site are obvious.*)

(d) Water that flows away from the site should not be visible. (*Once water has passed the building it has been used for cleansing, and as it is now polluted it may be the carrier of disease. Ideally, water flowing away from the site should go into the ground or under a bridge.*)

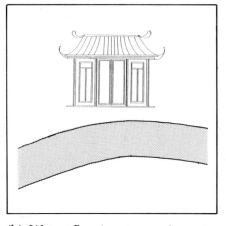

(b) Water flowing towards a site
(favourable)

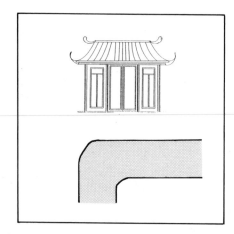

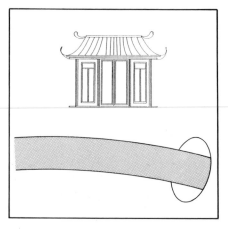

(c) Water flowing directly   (d) Water flowing away from a
towards a site (unfavourable)   site not visible (favourable)

(e) If water flows towards a site, and embraces the site by flowing around it, this is beneficial;

(f) but if water flows towards a site, then turns away from the site, benefits are brought, but not harvested.

(g) If water flows along the Tiger side of a site, from the Tortoise direction, then turns and flows in front of the house, this brings great fortune. (*This is often said to be the ideal Water Dragon, combining several Feng Shui precepts. The Water flows from the Tortoise side, symbolic of the Water element; it is flowing water, which stimu-*

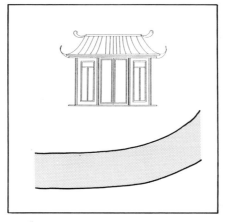

(e) Water embracing a site
(favourable)

(f) Water turning away from a
site (unfavourable)

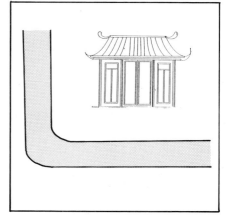

(g) Water flowing along the
Tiger side of a site (favourable)

lates ch'i; *it passes in front of the site, as a* Ming T'ang. *It only remains for the water flowing away to be hidden for the Water Dragon to be totally ideal.*)

(h) If water flows to a site, then turns, and in turning forms a deep pool through which the water flows, this signifies the accumulation of great wealth.

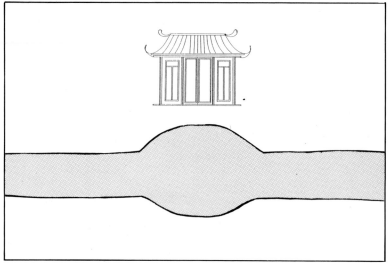

(h) Water forming a deep pool (favourable)

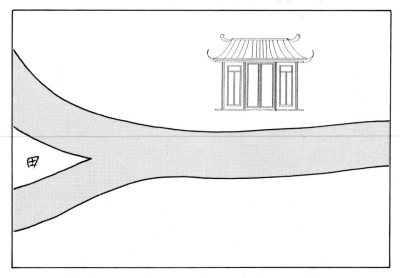

(i) Two confluences joining (favourable)

(i) Flowing water carries energizing *ch'i*; where one stream flows into another the *ch'i* are enhanced, and the spot is very favourable.

(j) Conversely, where a stream divides, the *ch'i* are also divided, and the benefits at either side are weakened.

(k) But the islet that is surrounded by water receives the full benefit of the *ch'i* on both sides.

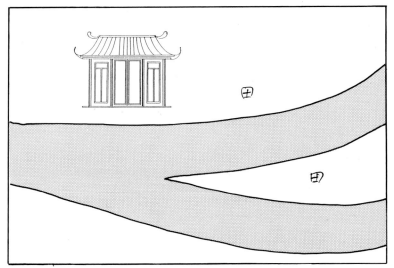

(j) A watercourse dividing (unfavourable)

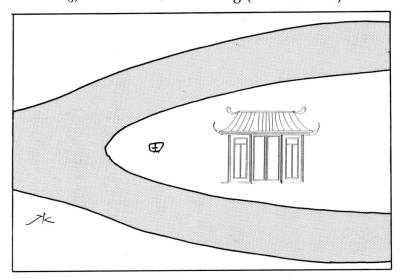

(k) Favourable and unfavourable sites by an islet

盤羅

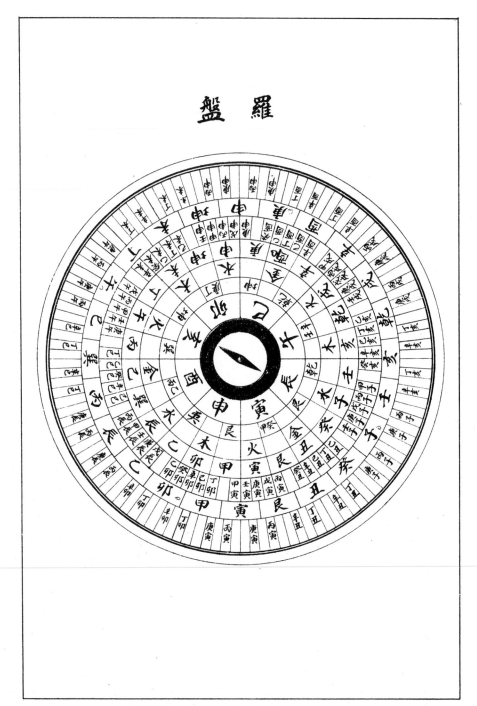

Chinese geomancer's compass

8

More Advanced Feng Shui

The reader has now been introduced to all the basic principles
of the art of Feng Shui. There is, however, one aspect of Feng
Shui that has not yet been mentioned: the Chinese geomancer's
compass. Readers who have encountered this unusual instrument
may be puzzled as to why an explanation of the function of such
an apparently essential tool has been left to such a late stage in
this book. There are a number of reasons for this. Firstly, the
geomantic compass only really comes into its own when the consultant has been invited to lay down the foundation lines for a
building that is still in the planning stage. Secondly, it tends to
be used more frequently for the orientation of graves, or 'dwellings for the dead' (not because the compass has any particularly
funereal function, but simply because, while few people can
afford to have a new house built, everyone eventually dies.) A
third, and very practical reason, is that even a simple descrip-
tion of the compass itself would be incomprehensible to anyone
who had not first obtained some basic knowledge of the art and
practice of Feng Shui.

Readers can now satisfy their curiosity with this brief descrip-
tion of the Chinese geomantic compass. Then, alas, it will be
necessary to go into the intricacies of the Chinese calendar and
unravel some of the deeper mysteries of the Chinese compass
before we can take a more in-depth look at the Chinese *Lo P'an*.

The *Lo P'an*

Lo means reticulated, like a net; *P'an* means a plate or dish. The
name is accurate; the surface of the inner dial of the *Lo P'an* is
covered with circles and divisions, giving the appearance of a cir-

cular net, or spider's web, while the dial itself, if removed from
its base, is actually bevelled like a plate or saucer. This saucer-
shaped dial sits in a depression in a square base plate, in which
it can be rotated. Most examples of *Lo P'an* seen in museums,
or as illustrated in books, are sadly lacking in the square base.
The base is quite plain, and apparently functionless, and museum
curators and others could perhaps be forgiven for thinking that
it was merely the box in which the dial came. This is far from
the case, but because the base plate is so simple in appearance
it can be described first.

The Base Plate

The base plate of the *Lo P'an* is square. It has a circular depression into which the dial sits loosely, enabling it to be rotated. The
base plate is fitted with two red threads, which run across the
face of the dial at right-angles, parallel to the sides of the square
base, and act as cursors. It is important that these threads are
accurately aligned with the sides of the base, crossing the pivot
of the compass needle, and firmly taut against the upper dial.

Because in the symbolism of *yin* and *yang* a square represents
the Earth, and a circle represents Heaven, the base plate is usually
referred to as the Earth Plate, and the dial as the Heaven Plate.
Inevitably this can be a source of great confusion, since the same
terms are also used for divisions of the dial itself.

The Dial Plate

The upper, or dial, plate of the *Lo P'an* is much more complex.
It is circular, with a bevelled cross-section, and sits in the depression in the base plate.

At its centre is a magnetic compass, the needle of which is
magnetized in such a way that it points south in accordance with
traditional Chinese cartographic usage.

A fine guide line is marked on the base of the compass needle
housing. Its appearance is so insignificant that this line usually
escapes the notice of the casual observer, but it has a vital function.

The compass needle in its housing is known as the 'Heaven
Pool'—possibly because this is the name of one of the constellations of Chinese astronomy close to the Pole Star, or because in

former times the compass needle floated on a drop of water.

The Reticulations

Beyond the Heaven Pool, and proceeding towards the edge of the dial, is a circular grid, divided into different numbers of divisions marked with Chinese characters.

The innermost divisions may be inscribed with the Eight Trigrams, or their Chinese names, or alternatively with the corresponding numbers of the Magic Square of Nine. In the latter case, the numbers are often represented as dots joined by lines, as if they were patterns of stars. Closer examination will reveal that in each case the order of the trigrams is that of the Former Heaven sequence, which is not the usual order for Chinese compasses. Their inclusion here is most likely intended to stress the fact that this is no ordinary mariner's or geographical compass, but one with special powers.

The number of rings on the dial varies according to the size and type of *Lo P'an*, but it would not be possible to explain the function of many of them until the reader was familiar with the Chinese compass plate.

Using the *Lo P'an*

When the *Lo P'an* is being used to assess the geomantic qualities of a site, the edge of the base plate is aligned with the walls of the building, or some other significant straight edge. The circular dial is then rotated until the guide line in the Heaven Pool is aligned with the compass needle. The operator then scrutinizes the dial, noting which signs on the dial fall under the red cursor thread.

Before the dial plate's divisions can be examined in closer detail, it is necessary to understand the language and function of the Chinese calendar.

The Chinese Calendar

Those who wish to make a deeper study of Feng Shui must have some knowledge of the Chinese calendar, because clients will often express a wish to know which days are likely to be the most propitious for the building of extensions, opening new wings, or even demolishing existing premises. The reader may think that this is more properly the province of the astrologer, but in general the twin disciplines of astrology and geomancy are rarely separated. Time and space are, as the reader will appreciate, inextricably linked.

NOTE: *Readers already conversant with the Chinese calendar through their knowledge of Chinese astrology should merely browse through the sub-headings of the following paragraphs until they reach an unfamiliar section.*

The Sexagenary Cycle (i): The Twelve Branches

It is well known that there is a Chinese 'zodiac' of twelve animals, which are used to reckon the years. The names of the animals were adopted about the seventh century by Buddhist monks as alternative popular names for twelve signs called the Twelve Branches.

The Twelve Branches are used to count, not only the years, but also the twelve months of the year, the twelve Chinese double-hours of the day, and even the days themselves.

The usual convention is to refer to the Twelve Branches by the roman numbers I to XII. Branch I represents the first year of the animal cycle, the year of the Rat. It also represents the first double-hour, of which midnight is the mid-point, and therefore lasts from 11 p.m. to 1 a.m.

For historical reasons, Branch I does not represent the first month of the Chinese year but the month that includes the Winter Solstice, two months before.

The Chinese have continuously numbered the days by twelves in regular sequence, without interruption, for several thousands of years. As an example, the first day of 1900 was Day XI; the first day of 2000 will be Day VII.

The Sexagenary Cycle (ii): The Ten Stems

Even older than the reckoning by the Twelve Branches is the sequence of Ten Stems. These appear to be the names of the days of a ten-day week. The names are extremely ancient, and most likely pre-date writing, since the symbols for the ten numbers appear on the very earliest examples of writing. The names of the earliest, semi-mythical emperors of China included the names of the stems, which suggests that they adopted the names of either the days when they were born or the days that they ascended the throne.

The convention for representing the stems is by the ordinary figures, 1 to 10. Thus, as well as a branch number, every day has a stem number. The stem for 1 January 1900 was 1; that for 1 January 2000 will be 5.

Stems and Elements

The Ten Stems match the Five Elements as follows:

1 *yang* Wood
2 *yin* Wood
3 *yang* Fire
4 *yin* Fire
5 *yang* Earth
6 *yin* Earth
7 *yang* Metal
8 *yin* Metal
9 *yang* Water
10 *yin* Water

Note that these ten figures are used here merely to identify the ten Chinese characters known as the Ten Stems. They must not be confused with mathematical numbers, which according to the *Lo Shu* have a different significance. But it is worth remembering that both Stem 5 and *Lo Shu* number 5 represent the element Earth.

The Chinese Compass Plate

The Chinese compass plate, as found on a traditional Chinese mariner's compass, does not divided the points of the compass successively by two, as does the familiar western compass. Once the four principal points have been sub-divided into the Eight Directions (North, North-east, etc), these eight directions further divide, uniquely, into twenty-four divisions. The curious system is based on the need of the astronomer to correlate the twelve divisions of the sky (marking the twelve months of the year, and

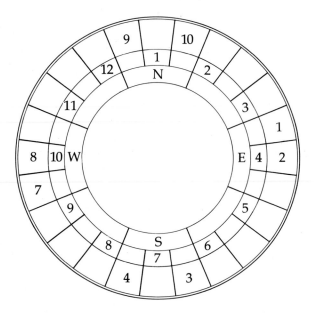

Evolution of the Chinese compass dial:
Innermost ring: Eight trigrams, or directions
Middle ring: The twelve branches, or months
Outermost ring: The ten stems, omitting 5 and 6

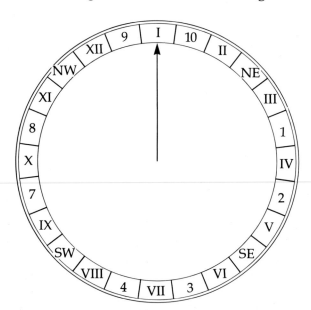

The twenty-four Chinese compass points

the twelve years of the Great Cycle of twelve years) with the twelve divisions of the clockface. Unfortunately, the clockface is not divisible into eight, so in order to distribute the Eight Directions equally with the twelve divisions the compass face is divided into twenty-four.

Four of the Eight Directions, the cardinal points, match the clockface positions, so the other four 'corner' directions, North-east, North-west, South-west, and South-east, are assigned to their appropriate places. This leaves eight positions so far unnamed. These are the positions on either side of the cardinal points.

Noting which stems are associated with the elements, we see that Stems 9 and 10 belong to Water, which is the element of the North. These two stems were therefore placed in the vacant positions either side of the North position, occupied by Branch I.

The reader who follows this reasoning will then see why 1 and 2 are placed either side of the East position at Branch IV, and Stems 3 and 4 either side of VII in the South, symbolizing Fire. In the West, symbolizing Metal, Stems 7 and 8 are placed at each side of Branch X. This leaves Stems 5 and 6 unaccounted for, which is appropriate since these stems are associated with the element Earth, representing the Centre.

The evolution of the Chinese compass plate is shown in the diagram above. The system may appear complex, but it is extremely ancient. An actual example of a diviner's board, showing the stems and branches in these positions, has been excavated from a tomb dating from the first or second century BC.

Repetition of the Compass Points

On most examples of *Lo P'an*, the twenty-four compass points are repeated twice, one ring 7½° clockwise, and the other 7½° anticlockwise of the principal orientation of the compass points. Various theories have been put forward to account for this repetition, including the possibility that the shifts represent an awareness of variations in the earth's magnetic field. The real reason derives from actual Feng Shui practice.

We shall see shortly that each of the twenty-four compass divisions is related to a particular Feng Shui 'star' as well as to other factors, such as the twenty-four solar fortnights. But also, the eight divisions of the compass relate to the eight orientations of a site.

Suppose that the orientation is Chinese compass direction Stem 10, to the West of true North. From the point of view of the Eight Trigrams, this orientation is the same as that for true North; but the equivalent divisions of the twenty-four point compass dial are out of alignment for Stem 10; accordingly, the geomancer consults that version of the compass ring which is shifted 7½° clockwise, in which true North is aligned with Stem 10.

The three arrangements of the compass dial are known by distinguishing names. The one aligned with true North is called the 'true needle'; the next ring, displaced 7½° anticlockwise, is the 'middle' needle (presumably on account of its having been placed between the true needle and the next); and the one displaced 7½° clockwise is the 'seam' needle.

Equating Compass Points with the Calendar

Since there are twenty-four compass points, each of these may be equated with one of the solar fortnights listed on p. 111, as well as with one of the hours of the western day.

The Chinese divide their twelve hours into twenty-four 'fore' and 'aft' 'little-hours'. Midnight marks the mid-point of Branch I (the Rat) double-hour, which lasts from 11 p.m. to 1 a.m. The first 'little-hour' of the day is therefore 11 p.m. till midnight; the second 'little-hour', midnight till 1 a.m.

The Twenty-Eight Lunar Mansions

The twenty-four solar fortnights enable the *Lo P'an* operator to find the earth's celestial position by compensating for its daily rotation with its annual orbiting of the sun. But it is not a very accurate system. Usually, on the edge of the *Lo P'an*, there is a ring of 365¼ divisions, one for each Chinese degree. Each degree therefore represents one day's change in the sun's position. By this means, the *Lo P'an* can also be used both as a terrestrial compass and a planisphere. For the latter purpose, next to the degree circle are marked the positions of the twenty-eight Chinese constellations that lie along the celestial equator. By noting the position of the full moon, which always occurs on the fifteenth day of the Chinese month, the operator is able to determine the sun's position among the stars, the full moon always occupying the part of the sky directly opposite to the sun. These factors enabled the olden-day Feng Shui professor to calculate the times and dates of eclipses, and the course of the solar year. The names of the twenty-eight constellations are listed below; they are considered to have a greater or lesser benign influence. It is possible to make a direct correlation between the dates of the western year and the degrees of the twenty-eight lunar mansions. The positions of the constellations, however, move by one degree, or day, every thirty years or so; *Lo P'an* of different periods alter positions of the twenty-eight mansions to account for this gradual change.* To digress beyond these introductory remarks on the use of the *Lo P'an* as an astronomical instrument would, however, be beyond the scope of this book.

THE TWENTY-EIGHT LUNAR MANSIONS†

MANSION			WIDTH (in degrees)	ASPECT
1	*Ch'io*	Horn	12	Favourable
2	*K'ang*	Neck	9	Unfavourable
3	*Ti*	Base	15	Unfavourable
4	*Fang*	Room	5	Favourable
5	*Hsin*	Heart	5	Unfavourable
6	*Wei*	Tail	18	Very favourable
7	*Chi*	Basket	11¼	Very favourable
8	*Tou*	Ladle	26	Favourable
9	*Niu*	Ox-boy	8	Unfavourable
10	*Nü*	Maiden	12	Unfavourable
11	*Hsü*	Void	10	Very unfavourable
12	*Wei*	Rooftop	17	Unfavourable
13	*Shih*	House	16	Favourable
14	*Pi*	Wall	9	Favourable
15	*K'uei*	Astride	16	Unfavourable
16	*Lou*	Mound	12	Very favourable
17	*Wei*	Stomach	14	Very favourable
18	*Mao*	Pleiades	11	Unfavourable
19	*Pi*	Net	16	Favourable
20	*Tsui*	Beak	2	Unfavourable
21	*Shen*	Orion	9	Variable

*For further remarks on the historical significance of the displacement of the positions of the twenty-eight lunar mansions on different examples of *Lo P'an*, see *Chinese Geomancy* (Element, 1989), p. 177.

†For further details on the twenty-eight lunar mansions, see *Chinese Astrology* (Aquarian Press, 1987), chapter 4; or *The Chinese Astrology Workbook* (Aquarian Press, 1988), pp. 65-77.

22	Ching	Well	33	Usually unfavourable
23	Kuei	Ghosts	4	Very unfavourable
24	Liu	Willow	15	Unfavourable
25	Hsing	Star	7	Usually unfavourable
26	Chang	Bow	18	Favourable
27	I	Wings	18	Unfavourable
28	Chen	Carriage	17	Favourable

The Twenty-Four Feng Shui Stars

In an earlier section (see p. 101) we saw how each division of a site had its own portent, depending on the direction it faced. In this section we shall see how each of the twenty-four compass points has its own star, or portent, depending on the orientation.

The twenty-four stars always follow the same order, but the position of the first star depends on the orientation of the site. The number of such orientations is eight—one for each trigram— not twenty-four, as might be supposed. Despite this, there are irregularities in establishing the position of the first star.

Once the positions of the twenty-four stars have been established, the portents for each of the twenty-four divisions of the compass can be shown. The effect of this is that more precise portents can be given for each direction. Thus, in cases when rooms are not aligned exactly with the Eight Directions, portents can be made for each room's precise orientation.

First, the names of the twenty-four stars and their portents:

1	Insanity	Poor
2	Mouth and Tongue	Can indicate scandal and gossip
3	Peace and Happiness	Excellent for health and family matters
4	Land and Dwelling	Good for those wishing to build
5	Weeping and Wailing	Disastrous
6	Orphan	Disastrous
7	Glory and Prosperity	Excellent for business and financial matters
8	Sorrowful Parting	Separation from loved ones; emigration
9	Debauchery	A scandalous life-style
10	Relatives in Marriage	Fortune through marriage
11	Joyous Pleasure	Great fortune
12	Disruption	Difficulties with plans
13	Prosperity and Wealth	Great fortune; success in business

14	Happiness and Virtue	Happiness, but not necessarily wealth
15	Sickness and Distress	Impending illness
16	Entering Wealth	The promise of a new career
17	Lengthy Illness	As the name suggests
18	Joyous Proclamation	Success in examinations, or official honours
19	Official of Prosperity	Success in management
20	Official of Honours	Examination successes, or success in sport or entertainment; public recognition
21	Breaker of Wealth	Loss of fortune
22	Commencing a Scroll	Change of career
23	Granting Happiness	Happiness at last
24	Execution Ground	Disgrace

To Find the Stellar Portent for Each Direction

First find the orientation of the site, according to the nearest of the Eight Directions.

Construct a circular compass chart, divided into twenty-four compartments, thus:

Refer to the orientation of the building: note the Orientation Number from this table:

TABLE OF ORIENTATION NUMBERS

North	10	South	13
North-east	4	South-west	3
East	22	West	9
South-east	11	North-west	16

Insert the Orientation Number into the lowest compartment of the chart (at the 'six-o'clock' position).

Ignore the remaining numbers in the table.

Proceeding clockwise from this point, complete with the numbers from 1 to 24 in the chart.

The chart now shows the numbers of the stellar portents for each of the twenty-four compass points.

Example

What is the stellar portent for a North-west facing room, in a house that faces West?

From the table, we see that the Orientation Number for a West-facing house is 9.
   Construct a compass chart (blank charts are provided on pp. 179 and 180).
   Insert the figure 9 in the lowest position, see figure opposite.
   Continuing clockwise, write the numbers 10 to 24 and 1 to 8 in the remaining spaces.

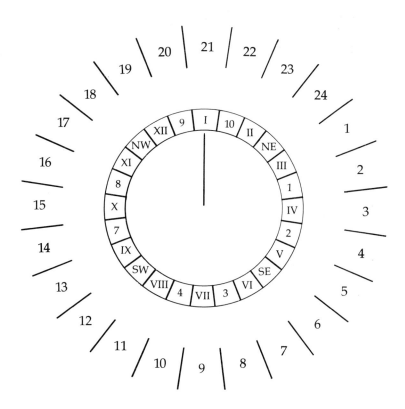

Note the figure at the North-west position.
   This is seen to be 18: the corresponding portent is Joyous Proclamation.

Exercise

Compile a compass chart for a South-east facing building, noting the portents.

Answer

Draw a chart and follow the working as before. The Orientation Number for South-east is 11, which appears at the 6 o'clock position in the completed chart. Your completed chart should appear as follows:

Blank chart for reader's use

Blank chart for reader's use

CHINESE COMPASS DIRECTION		STELLAR PORTENT	MEANING
	1	Insanity	Poor
	2	Mouth and Tongue	Can indicate scandal and gossip
	3	Peace and Happiness	Excellent for health and family matters
	4	Land and Dwelling	Good for those wishing to build
	5	Weeping and Wailing	Disastrous
	6	Orphan	Disastrous
	7	Glory and Prosperity	Excellent for business and financial matters
	8	Sorrowful Parting	Separation from loved ones; emigration
	9	Debauchery	A scandalous life-style
	10	Relatives in Marriage	Fortune through marriage
	11	Joyous Pleasure	Great fortune
	12	Disruption	Difficulties with plans
	13	Prosperity and Wealth	Great fortune; success in business
	14	Happiness and Virtue	Happiness, but not necessarily wealth
	15	Sickness and Distress	Impending illness
	16	Entering Wealth	The promise of a new career
	17	Lengthy Illness	As the name suggests
	18	Joyous Proclamation	Success in examinations, or official honours
	19	Official of Prosperity	Success in management
	20	Official of Honours	Examination successes, or success in sport or entertainment; public recognition
	21	Breaker of Wealth	Loss of fortune
	22	Commencing a Scroll	Change of career
	23	Granting Happiness	Happiness at last
	24	Execution Ground	Disgrace

9

Commercial Premises

In the Far East, the professional geomancer's time is divided roughly equally between advising on the layout of houses and apartments, the correct siting of graves so that ancestors may be at peace, and what is perhaps the principal source of remuneration, the best situation for commercial premises. Less than a year before these pages were being written, I met a high-ranking Chinese diplomat, who was intrigued to discover that a westerner should be so familiar with what is intrinsically a Chinese sub-

At Ping Tung, a professional geomancer checks the alignment of a grave, to ensure that ancestors will rest happily

ject. Very gently, he told me that in mainland China today Feng Shui and other 'superstitious practices' are no longer in existence. I nodded, but explained that in my experience, Feng Shui still flourished. I spoke of the *Lo P'an*, the geomantic compass, which I had bought in Yang Chou and which was of recent manufacture and made for local consumption. I also mentioned that I had a Chinese friend living in Hong Kong, who paid regular visits to China and subsisted on the generous gifts of clients who wanted Feng Shui advice. But in particular, I recounted my experience with the manager of a newly-built hotel in South China who had actually sent to Hong Kong for a geomancer in order to ensure that the alignments of the hotel were correct. The diplomat's eyes brightened.

'But of course,' he agreed, 'when Feng Shui is used to improve trade, then it is quite permissible.'

From these and subsequent remarks, I was able to deduce that for commercial premises, the Chinese of the post-revolutionary period were certainly not averse to calling upon the services of a geomancer to ensure that their trade would develop profitably; but Feng Shui for personal gain, the worship of ancestors, or its purely ritual function was severely censured.

The Hong Kong and Shanghai Bank, with its curiously askew

Even today, architects are obliged to follow the rules of Feng Shui, as the curious positioning of these escalators in the Hong Kong and Shanghai Bank building shows

geomantically placed escalators, is a well-known example of the influence of Feng Shui principles on commercial architecture; but less well know is the latest addition to the Hong Kong skyline; the Bank of China skyscraper, which, if one counts its telecommunications mast, is said to be the highest building in Asia. Hong Kong residents gleefully console themselves that the architects acting on behalf of their mainland China clients got their Feng Shui all wrong. The tall building is constructed from a series of triangular modules; and triangles, as everyone delightedly points out, are extremely bad Feng Shui.

But there is a well-known proverb that says a little knowledge is a dangerous thing. I find it highly unlikely that the bank's builders would be unaware of the importance of Feng Shui. I do not doubt for one moment that they would have consulted a geomancer when drawing up plans for Asia's tallest building. In my opinion, the Chinese architects knew exactly what they were doing. It stands among a forest of other skyscrapers, all of which, being tall and narrow, like the trunks of trees themselves, suggest the element of Wood. But the triangles of the Bank of China's building represent the element Fire; Wood feeds Fire, so the Bank of China is set to grow rich at the expense of the companies that surround it. The popular aversion to the triangle is a throwback to the days when most Chinese houses were built of wood, and as a consequence were more likely to fall victim to fire than today's concrete apartment blocks. Here, the lesson for the present student of Feng Shui is to be firmly grounded in the basic principles of Feng Shui before taking note of the everyday maxims that have evolved from them.

Assessing the Type of Premises

The basic principles that apply to the Feng Shui of commercial premises are no different from those that apply in the case of a house or a flat. Nor, in fact, is there any difference in their application. The only difference is in the function of the premises themselves. Some business premises will serve only one purpose, whether it is for design, manufacture, storage, point of sale, or whatever; but some premises will be used for all these functions. As in the domestic house, the various functions of the premises need to be defined first.

Let us look at some different examples of small businesses. We could take, as an example, a pharmacist's shop. The pharmacist has very little to do with either the design of the products or, presumably, with their manufacture. Storage, however, will be important, and probably there will be some dispensing and packaging to be done. The pharmacist will receive supplies, but is unlikely to dispatch many of them, save over the counter personally.

This is quite a different situation from the baker's shop. Here, baking might be done on the premises, and so manufacture is considered as one of the functions of the business. But even allowing for the kind of baker's retailing outlet that sells bread not baked on the premises, there is a significant difference. The baker's products are received and dispatched daily, and very little remains in store.

Compare this with a launderette. Here, the functions of delivery, dispatch, and storage are negligible, but the 'processing' is the chief function.

And, as a last example, we could consider an employment agency, which on the face of it has neither goods in, goods out, storage, nor manufacturing process to consider.

How do we apply the principles of Feng Shui to these widely differing kinds of business, if the same principles apply to all cases?

Bearing this question in mind, let us remind ourselves of two of the basic principles of Feng Shui: the Five Elements and the Eight Trigrams.

The Five Elements

There are many ways in which the influences of the Five Elements come to bear on assessing the Feng Shui possibilities of business premises. To begin with, we must see what element is most likely to prevail at that site. The ways of determining the most compatible element are no different from the methods that have already been outlined. By this, we must take note of the overall orientation of the building, the direction the entrance faces, and the appearance of the surroundings. Being commercial premises, it is most likely that the surroundings will be urban, and so it is the shape and nature of the surrounding buildings and their silhouettes that will be important. But it would not be unheard of for a business to be set up in quite rural surroundings—for example, for the manufacture of craft products, or perhaps the packaging of farm produce. In this case, the surrounding topography has to be taken into consideration, exactly as has been explained in the earlier chapters.

Secondly, it is important to reflect on the nature of the business and decide what element would be the most helpful, remembering that it is the element that *produces* the required element that will be the most beneficial to have predominantly present. So, in the first example, pharmaceuticals, which are creative and healing, suggest the element Wood. The Water element produces the Wood element, and consequently, it would be extremely beneficial for the pharmacy if the Water element was dominant; failing that, the Wood element would harmonize with the intentions of the business.

In the case of the bakery, Fire is the element suggested; consequently Wood, which produces Fire, would be a helpful element to have at that site.

In the third example, the element presiding over the launderette is obviously Water, so it would be hoped that either that element, or even better, Metal, which produces Water, would be the dominant element at the launderette's site.

Readers may be puzzled as to what element may best represent the employment agency in the fourth example. But Water is the element of communication, which is usually what such agencies are set up for; consequently it follows, perhaps surprisingly, that though the businesses of launderette and employment agency are so dissimilar, the same element conditions apply in both cases.

Of course, if the business is completely unsuited to the prevailing element (for example, if the site obviously came under the influence of Metal and the business was represented by the element Wood, as might happen, for example, if our prospective pharmacy was under a railway arch), then the geomancer would have to advise the client on ways in which the malevolent influences could best be deflected or neutralized. Again, the same kind of advice would be given as if the prevailing element did not match the ideal element for domestic dwelling. Some suggestions are given on pp. 153-7 ('Rectifying an Imbalance of Elements'), but there will be other remedies that would only apply to certain commercial and industrial situations.

The Eight Trigrams

Once the site is established, and the business is set up, the next stage is to decide how to make the best use of the space available.

All work is change: the mason changes the shape of stone, the builder changes the position of bricks, the tailor changes the shape of cloth, the chemist changes the nature of substances, the doctor changes the constitution of one's health, the taxi-driver changes our personal location, the miner changes the place of coal, the teacher changes the limits of our understanding.

The Eight Trigrams, the core of the ancient classic called the *Book of Changes* (the *I Ching*), are the key to change. Thus, as it is through the Eight Trigrams that all change is effected, the Eight Trigrams are the means by which all work is carried out and, as a further consequence, they are the key to the prosperity of any business. From a Feng Shui point of view, it is therefore essential that all work proceeds at a location that comes under the auspices of its most appropriate trigram.

As in the case of a house or flat, first make a rough plan of the premises, then allocate the trigrams to their respective directions. This identifies the type of work that might best be performed in that area. Next, taking the orientation of the building into account, as before, note the auspices of each direction to see which parts of the building (or floor space) are beneficial and which are less successful. The procedure for this is exactly the same as outlined in the earlier section 'The Eight Orientations' (p. 98).

Once comparative charts have been drawn up, it will be seen that certain areas will be appropriate for particular aspects of the business, but not for others. Of course, when the Eight Auspices are calculated, the areas most appropriate for the business in hand may be found to be unsuitable. It is easiest to give an actual example.

Suppose that the business under consideration was a garage mechanic's repair shop and that the premises faced North-west. Now it will be seen from the list of activities appropriate for each trigram that the trigram *K'an*, North, is concerned with circular motion, ideal for business involving wheels and mechanics. But the premises, facing North-west, is of the *Ch'ien* type, in which the ideal North position is occupied by the auspice 'Six Curses'—hardly encouraging. Obviously, this orientation is definitely unsuited for a business whose principal functions are mechanics and engineering. But that does not mean to say that the premises cannot be used for any other kind of business. In the South-west position is the auspice 'Lengthened Years', while the trigram *K'un*, corresponding to the South-west position, is appropriate for medical centres and welfare. Such an orientation would therefore be ideal for the pharmacist's shop.

Having established whether or not the orientation is appropriate for the business, the next stage is to divide the area itself. Certain areas will be badly aspected, but it may be that the layout of the premises (if say, the floorplan is of an irregular shape) cuts out those areas that fall under the influence of the worse aspects.

This is when it is essential to identify the relative importance of the different functions of the business. Above, we saw how four different businesses placed greater or lesser emphasis on different aspects that are common to all commercial enterprises. If, say, distribution is an important factor of the business, then it is important to ensure that the orientation of the premises is one in which the auspices that affect the East position are fortunate, since the trigram *Chen* (the East) officiates over speed, roads, and distribution generally. The reader will see that the orientation *K'an* (North), *Sun* (South-east), and *Li* (South) all have favourable auspices in the East position.

If we summarize the four examples of businesses given above, we can see the relative importance of the various stages of the commercial process.

TYPE OF BUSINESS	PHARMACY	BAKERY	LAUNDERETTE	AGENCY
Goods in	*	**		
Processing	*	****	**********	
Counter service	***	**	*	***
Storage	****			
Distribution		*		
Communications				*******
Cash point	***	***	*	*

This table enables us to see that it is not only the emphasis on different aspects of activity that varies from business to business; the range of activities also varies. The pharmacy and the bakery have several aspects that have to be considered as relatively important; but the launderette and the employment agency have a much narrower spectrum of priorities to consider. It might easily happen that the orientation of the premises, being badly sited, had few areas with beneficial auspices but one essential area that happened to be auspicious for a business such as the launderette or the agency which concentrated on one particular activity. Other businesses might benefit from having a generally benevolent influence all round, rather than one highly auspicious area.

The Eight Types of Activity

The eight types of change manifested by the Eight Trigrams determine the kind of commercial activity to which they are most appropriate. These can be summarized as follows:

K'an—NORTH
Change of direction
Circular motion

   Hence: rotation; drills; lathes; stationary engines; machines and mechanical engineering.

   K'an is also the symbol of danger and dangerous activity, which might be associated with circular saws, drills, and the like. If this is the focal point of the business, it should be well aspected. Avoid the auspices: Severed Fate, Accident and Mishap, and Six Curses. Five Ghosts could be tolerated if the engineering side were only a minor part of the business.

Ken—NORTH-EAST
No change.
Barriers; immutability.

   Hence: immobility; gates; security; storage; safes; strong-rooms.

   This area is ideally suited either for a secure premises, or for the storage of perishables or valuables.

Chen—EAST
Change of place.
Linear movement (as distinct from the circular motion of the trigram *Ken*.

   Hence: roads; transport; speed; distribution. Ideal for despatch, transport.

In manufacturing, this is suitable for production line processes, which involve cumulative change.

Sun—SOUTH-EAST
Change of form.
Continuity.
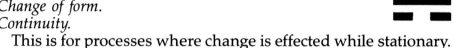
This is for processes where change is effected while stationary. Suitable for slow, painstaking processes, as well as routine work.

Li—SOUTH
Change of substance.
Fire.
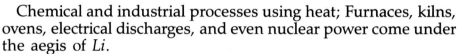
Chemical and industrial processes using heat; Furnaces, kilns, ovens, electrical discharges, and even nuclear power come under the aegis of *Li*.

K'un—SOUTH-WEST
Biological change.
Nourishment.
Hence: gentle generative processes. Suitable for laboratory culture growths, seed germination, and all biological processes.

In an industrial complex, the ideal position for the welfare area, or the staff canteen.

Tui—WEST
Psychological change.
Reflections.
Ideal for all matters connected with entertainment and recreation, rather than actual manufacturing processes. Suitable for the maintenance of musical instruments, scientific instrument calibration, and delicate measurement.

Ch'ien—NORTH-WEST
Creative change
Strength; expansion; creativity.
All matters connected with the initiative processes: design, management, and leadership.

The Portents

Exactly as in the case of a house or flat, the positions of the portents change according to the orientation of the building. The reader is reminded that the name of the unfavourable portents are:

Six Curses
Five Ghosts
Severed Fate
Accident and Mishap

and the favourable ones:

Lengthened Years
Generating Breath
Celestial Monad

The entrance to the building, which occupies the eighth direction, will be discussed in a later section.

When planning the work area, consideration should be given not only to deciding which direction is the most appropriate for that particular activity, but also to whether the area is likely to be prosperous or not. The reader should refer to these notes for suggestions on making the best use of the available space.

There is a slight difference in the way that the portents are considered when the case in question concerns business premises rather than a domestic dwelling. To take an example, while the Five Ghosts may not be welcome in one's bedroom, it does not matter a great deal if a particular work station is haunted: the only people likely to suffer are those who might sleep on the job. An ideal location, one might think, for the night watchman's hut! On the other hand, while in a residence one would like to have Lengthened Years in the bedroom or living room areas (these being the areas of the house that are occupied longest), it might be more appropriate in the case of certain businesses for 'dead' areas, such as storerooms, to be protected by the auspices of Lengthened Years if the storage of perishable goods was an integral part of the business.

We shall now consider each of the seven kinds of portents in turn, and see what parts of the business complex might be best suited to them.

Six Curses

It was explained in an earlier section that the Six Curses portend irritations and setbacks. These are hardly encouraging signs for the smooth running of a business. The manager should decide what part of the running of the concern would be likely to prove the least damaging if the Six Curses were influential. The most advisable course of action might be to put the staff canteen or rest-rooms here, always provided, of course, that staff relations would not suffer as a result.

POSITIONS OCCUPIED BY THE SIX CURSES FOR EACH ORIENTATION

Entrance facing	*Six Curses*
North	North-west
North-east	East
East	North-east
South-east	West
South	South-west
South-west	South
West	South-east
North-west	North

Five Ghosts

The disposition of the Five Ghosts is not likely to be a problem in the case of a factory or commercial premises that closes down at night. Security staff might feel a little insecure at patrolling an area that had the reputation of being haunted, but in China the course of action is always to place a shrine at the position of the Five Ghosts, not only to appease the spirits, but also to solicit their co-operation. When Chinese managers find that one specific area of the factory proves troublesome, with numerous untoward or inexplicable accidents occurring, a geomancer is often called in. If the problem is that the area is occupied by the Five Ghosts, and they are not being appeased by the token shrine, the only solution is to exorcise them. This negative area might also be advantageously used for the rest-rooms, as it might discourage their over-use!

POSITIONS OCCUPIED BY THE FIVE GHOSTS FOR EACH ORIENTATION

Entrance facing	Five Ghosts
North	North-east
North-east	South-east
East	North-west
South-east	South-west
South	West
South-west	South-east
West	South
North-west	East

Severed Fate

This is a highly inauspicious area; frankly, it signifies grave physical danger. On no account should the area be used for heavy or dangerous machinery, or dangerous processes, without the strictest safety precautions being taken. It would be far better for this area to be used for storage, also making sure that items are stored sensibly and safely.

POSITIONS OCCUPIED BY THE SEVERED FATE FOR EACH ORIENTATION

Entrance facing	Severed Fate
North	South-west
North-east	South
East	West
South-east	North-east
South	North-west
South-west	North
West	East
North-west	South

Accident and Mishap

This is yet another area liable to accidents, although the result may not be as grave as for those who fall victim to the malevolent influences of the Severed Fate. This area should be avoided for processes involving cutting, the use of sharp implements, and other hazardous tasks.

POSITIONS OCCUPIED BY ACCIDENT AND MISHAP FOR
EACH ORIENTATION

Entrance facing	*Accident and Mishap*
North	West
North-east	West
East	South-west
South-east	North-west
South	North-east
South-west	East
West	North
North-west	South-east

Lengthened Years

This is one of the most favourable auspices. The best use of this
portent is for the director's suite, or the accountancy offices, to
be placed here, to ensure the continuing prosperity and well-being
of the firm. But as was said in the introduction to this section,
if the business involves the storage of perishable or highly valuable goods, this would also be the ideal place for the cold storage
or strong rooms. In most cases, however, storage rooms would
be placed in a position where baleful influences were unlikely
to have a great effect.

POSITIONS OCCUPIED BY LENGTHENED YEARS FOR EACH
ORIENTATION

Entrance facing	*Lengthened Years*
North	South
North-east	South-west
East	South-east
South-east	East
South	North
South-west	North-west
West	North-east
North-west	South-west

Generating Breath

This is one of the most creative positions. If the firm relies for
its success on being up-to-date with new ideas, this area would
be used to great advantage by the design studio. If the manner
of the business was to produce work to order, however, and the
creative side was of less importance, this area should be used
for the accountancy and management suite, the Generating Breath

being channelled to develop the financial well-being of the business.

POSITIONS OCCUPIED BY THE GENERATING BREATH FOR EACH ORIENTATION

Entrance facing	Generating Breath
North	South-east
North-east	North-west
East	South
South-east	North
South	West
South-west	North-east
West	North-west
North-west	West

Celestial Monad

This is a generally favourable area, its sphere of influence being broad rather than specific. This area should be allocated to what the business regards as its second or third most important function. Routine work, administration, dispatch of goods, in fact all matters subservient to the prime purpose of the business will all run smoothly in the area occupied by the Celestial Monad.

POSITIONS OCCUPIED BY THE CELESTIAL MONAD FOR EACH ORIENTATION

Entrance facing	Celestial Monad
North	West
North-east	North
East	North
South-east	South
South	South-east
South-west	West
West	South-west
North-west	North-east

Ch'i and Sha

The previous sections of this chapter dealt with the technical applications of Feng Shui to commercial premises—what might properly be called an investigation of the concern's Feng Shui according to the principles of the Compass School. Now we take a general approach to the business, and consider its Feng Shui from the viewpoint of the Form School. In looking at business premises, we have the same considerations that we have when we investigate a domestic dwelling; it is just that the emphasis, particularly in the channelling of the *ch'i*, is rather different.

We begin first by looking at the doors and windows. Again, we have to consider the business, and what is actually the function of the doors and windows. The answer is not as obvious as it might seem. When we looked at the four examples of businesses in the previous (Compass School) section, we saw the great difference in emphasis that a pharmacy, a bakery, a launderette, and an employment agency gave to various stages of the enterprise. Now we can look at the differences in function of four more High Street businesses; a greengrocer's, a furniture shop, a jeweller's, and a bank.

First, take the matter of the door. At the greengrocer's, the door is hardly apparent. Often, many of the goods are displayed on the street; the doors are wide open, since the fresh air helps to keep the goods cool and prolongs their saleable life. It is, therefore, a *yang* or open type of shop, and customers are hardly aware that they have crossed the threshold when they pick up goods they want.

Now take the case of the furniture shop. Here, big display windows show off the large and bulky products; but in order to protect the goods, which are probably more than a hundred times more valuable than the greengrocer's, the doors have to be kept closed against the weather. Again, however, it is an open shop, where customers wander among the goods, but with a further difference; the customers can hardly pick up the chairs and tables and take them home on the spot.

Now to the jeweller's. Generally speaking, the value of the goods sold here will be the same as the items sold by the furnishers, but the jeweller can hardly be expected to let customers browse round and handle the watches, rings and brooches indiscriminately. Although the windows will display the goods, they are much smaller. And the doors not only shut out the weather, they may also shut out the casual passer-by, and only be opened on request. This is a *yin* closed type of shop.

Finally, the bank. This may not have any windows at all, and such doors as it has will be large, impressive, and secure when shut. There might be a little advertising, to canvass our attention for the bank's interest rates, but there are no goods on display. This again, is a closed type of business.

In considering the flow of *ch'i* through a business premises, the type of business has to be taken into account, since this not only affects the way in which the *ch'i* will be channelled, but also, the more open the shop, the more susceptible it will be to attacks from adverse *sha*.

The Entrance

Firstly, it must be ensured that no straight lines in the form of paths or corners of buildings are directed at the entrance. If this is the case, there are several ways to overcome 'secret arrows' and other adverse influences. Mirrors deflect straight lines and have the additional advantage of brightening the shop's interior, as well as giving an enhanced impression of the stock.

Another useful ploy is to set the store of goods at a convenient angle; perhaps in a diamond shape, which has the added purpose of persuading the customers to circulate round the displays. Much depends on the type of goods being sold, however.

The theme of setting the interior at an angle has a variant form often used by banks and jewellers, which is to set the door at an angle. The origin of this feature was a means of re-orienting the entire buildiing at the least expense. If, for example, the premises were of the *Ch'ien* or North-west type, but the most suitable orientation for the type of business was North, then the entrance would be recessed and the door set at an angle so that it faced North—thus completely altering the positioning of the portents without having to rebuild the entire premises.

In time, it was generally thought that the simple artifice of setting a door at an angle guaranteed good Feng Shui, and it became commonplace to adopt this architectural fashion as a matter of course, without fully understanding the original reason. One Hong Kong bank invariably sets the entrances to its branch offices at a corner, and it is popularly supposed that this is for good Feng Shui rather than design reasons.

A benefit of setting the entrance in a porch at an angle is that potential customers are often drawn into the unenclosed part of the entrance—the porch area—to examine the goods in the shop window, without the customer actually having to enter the shop itself. This is of particular advantage for businesses of the closed type (such as a jeweller's) where it is not customary for passers-by to wander round and browse.

Through the Doors

After the orientation of the entrance has been established, it is important to consider the doors themselves. While public buildings, because of safety regulations, are obliged to have outwardly-opening doors, there is no doubt that doors that opened into the visitor's face would be actively discouraging. Most house doors open inwards, and the Form School geomancers all agree that this encourages beneficial *ch'i* to enter the house. But in the case of premises which are obliged to have outwardly opening doors it might be prudent to have such doors provided for safety purposes while the actual entrance itself had inwardly-facing ones. When the design of the building does not lend itself to the provision of two sets of doors, attention might be given to the provision of swing doors, revolving doors, or even that useful oriental invention, the sliding door.

Once inside the building, the visitor encounters the first difference between business and a residential premises. Commercial premises, during their hours of business, are open to the public. Visitors may be actively encouraged to wander in uninvited and examine the goods on sale. Banks, agencies, and wholesalers may have more restricted access, and potential clients may in some cases only arrive by appointment. Whatever the case, from the greengrocer to the merchant bank, the aim is to make a good initial impression on the visitor, whether by the variety and quality of the goods on display, or by the efficiency and managerial skills of the less public type of business.

Chinese commercial concerns often install indoor gardens, usually with ornamental pools and fish, at the point of reception, the plants and water stimulating beneficial *ch'i*. The more enclosed the type of entrance, the more important it is to generate stimulating *ch'i*. Of course, the placing of plants (Wood), fish (Fire), ornamental rocks (Earth), or pools (Water) may also be the means to correct an imbalance of elements at a critical point. Thus, their function serves to correct an adverse Feng Shui condition both from the point of view of the Form School, as well as of the Compass School.

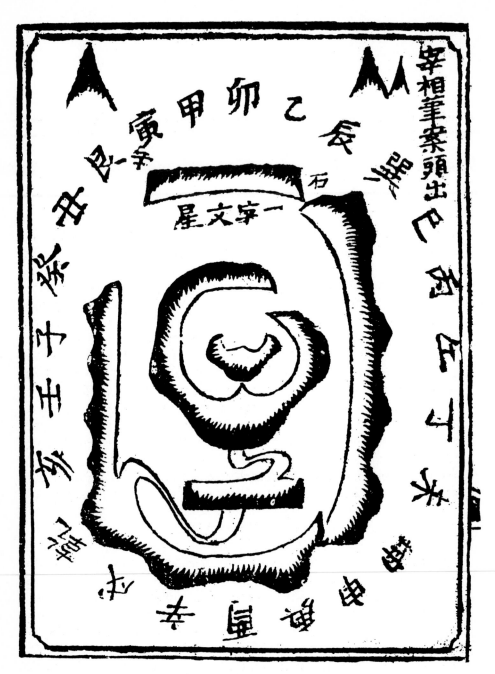

Example of a Chinese Feng Shui map

10

A Feng Shui Survey of Your Home

The reader has now been introduced to the fundamental principles of the two schools of Feng Shui—the Form School, which looks at the relationship of a particular place to its surroundings, and the Compass School, which considers the implications of the way in which a building is oriented. I imagine that many readers, after completing the set examples of this book, will have wanted to try the calculations out for themselves, using their own personal data. Now that the theory behind all the practical work has been covered, it is important to draw all the threads together and set out a complete summary of all the points dealt with in this book, not so much in the order of the various principles as they have been set out, but in the order that would be most practical for someone carrying out a Feng Shui survey of some particular premises.

This chapter therefore sets out the kind of information you need and reminds you of the way to carry out your Feng Shui survey.

Initial Procedure

Your aim will be to complete a geomantic survey of some premises, and to this end sample Geomantic Survey Charts are given on pp. 211 and 218-19. Some of the pages are to help you with your notes and calculations, while others are for the completed geomantic survey. You can use the charts in this book, or design your own. If you wish to avoid writing in this book, make copies of the relevant pages. In any case, you will need a notebook, pencil, and an ordinary compass.

If the survey is for yourself, you could being by filling in the name of the client and the location of the premises on the charts straightaway. You might even have prepared the groundwork for the later technicalities, by calculating data such as the Natal Numbers and entering them on the charts. If you are preparing the charts for someone else, and you already have this information, it is a good idea to get this done before you begin the survey. However, we shall imagine that the geomancer has been called to do a Feng Shui of some premises and that the information is not yet available.

On Arrival at the Site

Note the direction of magnetic North with an ordinary compass.

Lay this on the chart of the Chinese compass dial (p. 170) so that you are familiar with the direction of the twenty-four Chinese compass points.

On a notepad, list all the topographical and architectural features visible from the site. Note their compass bearing, according to one of the twenty-four Chinese compass points.

A list of features is given on p. 18ff. In particular, look for:

> Distant hills
> Water (streams, lakes, canals, ponds)
> Tall trees
> Open spaces
> Pillars, posts
> Arches
> Tall buildings
> The nature of roofs
> Roads leading directly to the premises
> Telephone wires
> Any other distinctive features

Comment and advise
If there are any features which constitute adverse sha *or beneficial* ch'i, *note these particularly. In the event of the former, be prepared to suggest how they might be eliminated. This topic is covered at length in earlier chapters of this book.*

Identify, if possible, the location of the Dragon, Bird, Tiger, or Tortoise.

Comment and advise.
Find the position of the Dragon if possible, or the other features by default. If they can be readily identified, advise the client of the potential benefit. Make every effort to identify their location as it is a negative attitude to advise a client that the location, from a Feng Shui point of view, is not ideal.

If the house is a terraced house, or semi-detached, so that one or more walls are adjoining other premises, make a note of this. Note which walls are so joined, for these will block any Feng Shui influences, good or bad, at those sides.

If so, comment and advise.
When drawing up the orientation chart (see later) draw a line right across the quarter of the chart which is blocked by the adjoining house. Any Feng Shui features on that side may be ignored, unless they are visible from an upper storey, or part of the house, such as a kitchen extension or conservatory, which does not join on to the neighbouring building.

Stand at the entrance to the premises and note the orientation of the house according to one of the Eight Directions. Note whether the path that leads up to the entrance approaches the premises face on, at an angle, at a curve, or sideways.

Comment and advise.
Paths should not come directly up to the house. Suggest alternative routes for the path if this be the case.

On Entering the Premises

Note whether the door opens inwards, allowing the *ch'i* to enter.

Comment and advise.
It is very unusual for the main entrance door to open outwards. If it does, suggest that it be rehung, or another entrance considered as the main entrance.

If there is a porch with two doors, note whether both doors hang on the same side.

Comment and advise.
Doors should open in the same direction and at the same side. It
is actually physically awkward and impractical for doors to open
in different directions.

Note whether both doors are properly aligned.

Comment and advise.
If it is impossible, because of the fabric of the building, to have them
properly aligned, suggest that strips of mirror are put alongside the
inner door.

Note whether the stairs approach the door and whether a rear
door may be seen from the front door.

If so, comment and advise.
In both cases, a curtain or screen may be placed between the front
door and the rear door to prevent the loss of ch'i.
   In the case of the stairs, a common Chinese remedy is to place
talismans, or guardian deities, at the head of the stairs or on a half-
landing. But the installation of a shrine is best left until the posi-
tion of the Five Ghosts has been calculated.

Surveying the Rooms

The following are general points that apply to every room in the
house.

Note the direction faced by the windows.

Comment and advise.
Are there any favourable features, such as the Dragon or Tiger, that
can be seen from the window? Conversely, is the room overlooked
by features that produce harmful influences? The furnishings of the
room should take these into account.

Note whether any windows are directly opposite the door.

Comment and advise.
Windows opposite the door permit the escape of beneficial ch'i before
they have had the opportunity to circulate.

Note whether any windows are directly opposite each other.

> *Comment and advise.*
> *Remember that windows opposite each other produce an instability within the room. Suggest ways of introducing a focal point.*

Note the position of overhead beams.

> *Comment and advise.*
> *Despite their popularity as authentic touches in period houses, overhead beams are considered to have adverse geomantic properties. Advise that furniture is placed away from such beams. In small bedrooms, where it may not be possible to place the bed without it being under a beam, ensure that the beam runs the length, rather than across the bed.*

Further Remarks on Particular Rooms

Each room in the house has its own particular purpose, which demands certain criteria that may not be important for another room. The following remarks can be borne in mind as each room is visited in turn.

The Living-room

Note the flow of the *ch'i*.

> *Comment and advise.*
> *The beneficial ch'i should flow through this room gently, in order to promote domestic harmony and prosperity. It is also important that, when calculating the Eight Portents, the auspices for this room should be one of the most fortunate.*

Note the outlook from the windows.

> *Comment and advise.*
> *The room should have a pleasant outlook, and not be overshadowed by the house: accordingly, a southerly aspect is most favourable. As the room is most likely to be used in the afternoons or evenings, a westerly outlook is also favoured.*

Note any irregularity in the shape of the room.

> *Comment and advise.*
> *If the shape of the room is irregular, calculate the portents and, by using a screen or room divider, partition off the limb of the room that is most unfavourable.*

Note the positioning of the chairs.

> *Comment and advise.*
> *The chair used by the head of the household should not have its back to a window or a door, the obvious reason being that such a position renders the person vulnerable to intruders. The Chinese prefer the furniture to follow the lines of the four walls; preferably, no chair should have its back to a window or door, but be placed sideways to them. If this is not possible, position a mirror so that the door may be seen from the chairs.*
>
> *The head of the household would normally face South, and an honoured guest would be placed in the same position.*

The Dining-room

When the family sit at the table together, they should be seated according to the relative positions of the Eight Trigrams. The positions at an eight-sided table may be deduced from the tables in the Trigrams chapter (p. 95). At a long table, the positions will be as follows:

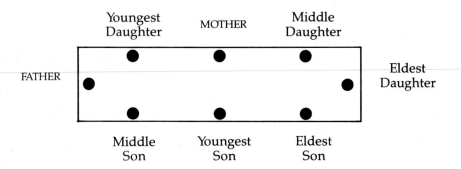

Note the direction faced by the window, and the location of the dining-room.

Comment and advise.
It is said that the window of the dining-room should face a different
direction from the location of the dining-room itself, in order to stimu-
late the flow of ch'i. *This implies that the dining-room should be*
at a corner of the house. Thus, if the dining-room is in the South
part of the house, the windows should not look southwards, but
eastwards, or westwards.

The Kitchen

Most accidents happen in the home, and then primarily in the
kitchen.
  Note the position of the stove, and the water supply.

Comment and advise.
It is very important that the kitchen is not located in an area that
comes under the jurisdiction of one of the malevolent portents such
as Accident and Mishap. The danger from the element Fire is at
once obvious, while the element Metal may threaten through the
kitchen's battery of knives and sharp kitchen implements. Ensure
that the stove (representing the element Fire) adjoins neither the
element Water nor Wood. Being next to Wood, the danger of Fire
is enhanced. Being placed next to Water produces the Chinese charac-
ter meaning 'disaster'.
  Instead, ensure that the stove is insulated, symbolically if not prac-
tically, from the sinks and water supply by interposing features
representing the elements Earth or Metal (such as store cupboards
for pots and pans, for example).

The Bathroom

A building's North side, being sympathetic to the element Water,
is an appropriate location for the bathroom. But it is important
to note which portent pertains to the North side of the premises;
if the portent is Accident and Mishap, special attention should
be given to the use of this room by young children and the elderly.
  Popular Feng Shui principles hold that the bathroom should
not lead into the bedroom, the explanation for this precept being
that in bedrooms a smooth gentle flow of *ch'i* is required, while
in bathrooms it is important to displace the sullied *ch'i* as quickly
as possible.

According to the principles of Feng Shui, when Water leaves a site, it should be unseen—a reminder that all drains and culverts leaving the bathroom (and kitchen) should be completely covered.

Note the position of the bathroom, and other features.

Comment and advise.

The Bedroom

A greater proportion of one's life is spent in the bedroom than in any other part of the house; accordingly, the location of the bedroom is crucial. More so than any other room, the bedroom must be compatible with the Feng Shui horoscopes of its occupants.

Note the outlook of the windows.

Comment and advise.
For young people, the window may look East, so that they may receive the full benefit of the rising sun's energizing force; for elderly people it is better for the window to receive the gentler rays of the setting sun. A South-facing bedroom loses all the benefits of the sun's yang influence, since it is not occupied during the day; a North-facing bedroom never receives the influence at all.

Note the position of the bed.

Comment and advise.
It should not receive direct sunlight, since the excess of yang force disturbs sleep. The same is true of mirrors; too many mirrors produce an over-abundance of stimulating ch'i, while the bed should not face a mirror lest the spirit catch sight of its reflection when it rises for its nocturnal perambulations.
*   The bed must not face the door, as this has too close an association with funerals, since the corpse is carried out feet first.*

The Study

Studies are nearly always a clutter of books, curios, and the curious impedimenta of research. It is important, however, to try and retain one area as a *Ming T'ang* or a reserve pool of quietude.

Chinese scholars believe that scrolls depicting mountains and water bring inspiration, while every writer's desk aspires to support a seal, ink-slab, or pen-rest in the shape of a miniature carving of a weathered rock to represent the Dragon of the mountains.

Note any specific features of the study.

Comment and advise.

The Workshop

The workshop holds as many hazards as the kitchen, if not more. According to the Eight Trigrams, its ideal location is North, as this is represented by *K'an*, the symbol of circular motion—perhaps because the workshop does not need the sun's light, perhaps because the North Pole is the axle of the earth's rotation. But if the workshop is in frequent use, it would be dangerous for it to be situated in a position occupied by the portents Accident and Mishap or Severed Fate as these would be more than usually ominous where there were drills, circular saws, lathes, and other potentially lethal tools.

Note any specific features of the workshop.

Comment and advise.

Completing the Survey Charts

The groundwork for the geomantic survey having been made, the information can now be transferred to the charts. Before doing so, ascertain the dates of birth of each of the members of the household.

Turn to the Geomantic Survey Chart (Chart 1) overleaf. Complete the headings by inserting the names of the chief householder and other members of the family, and their dates of birth. Insert the address of the premises and from your notes 'On Arrival at the Site' insert the orientation of the house.

From your notes 'On Arrival at the Site' you can begin to complete a 'Location Chart'. A sample Location Chart (Chart 2) is provided on p.211, and a blank chart (Chart 3) on p.212. Insert the features you have noted into the blank spaces on the chart, in accordance with their compass directions.

GEOMANTIC SURVEY CHART (Chart 1)

Head of household _____
Date of Birth _____

Second principal member of household _____
Date of birth _____

Other members of household _____

    _____

    _____

    _____

    _____

    _____

Address of premises _____

    _____

Orientation _____

Note the orientation of the premises from Chart 1.

In the eight-division features circle, note the position of the entrance, and from the chart on p. 213, complete the blank spaces in the outermost ring with the names of the Portents.

Make an approximate outline of the ground plan of the house, and sketch this in the centre of the chart, ensuring that the entrance faces the appropriate one of the Eight Compass Directions on the inner ring of the chart.

According to the orientation of the premises, find the South Stellar Portent number from this table:

North	10	South	13
North-east	4	South-west	3
East	22	West	9
South-east	11	North-west	16

Insert the South Stellar Portent into the chart at the South Point of the chart (marked with a ▲). Insert the remaining numbers from 1 to 24 so that they run clockwise. This completes the Stellar Portent Numbers.

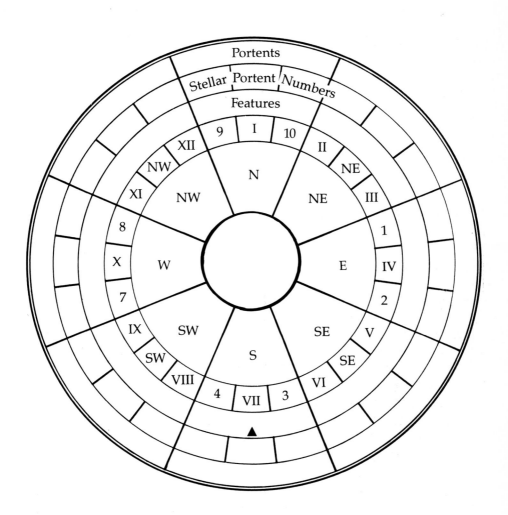

SAMPLE LOCATION CHART (Chart 2)

LOCATION CHART
(Chart 3)

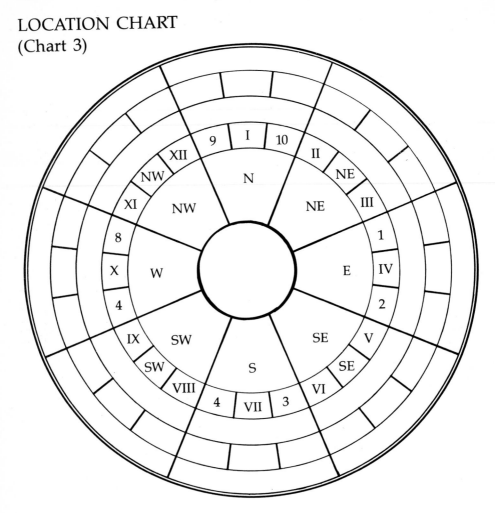

Complete the Personal Feng Shui and Rooms Charts (Charts 5 and 6) noting the relative location of the rooms in the premises. From the Portents (Chart 4), and the Personal Chart (Chart 5), note which rooms are favourable, and to which member of the family they are best suited.

Once the charts have been completed (see sample completed chart on p. 215; additional blank charts for your use appear on pp. 218-223), you should return to your notes and summarize the observations you have made in the form of a report, along the lines of the suggestions outlined above.

Always ensure that you draw attention to the better points of the Feng Shui; where your observations lead you to the conclusion that the Feng Shui is unfavourable you should be practical in the advice that you proffer.

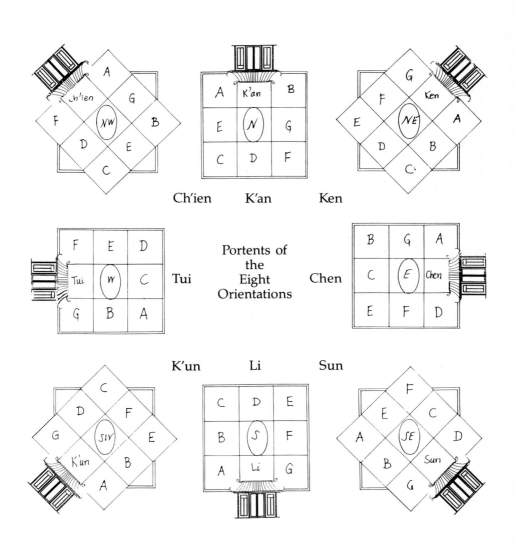

PORTENTS CHART (Chart 4)

PERSONAL FENG SHUI CHART (Chart 5)

First Resident:
Name _____
Birthdate _____
Sex: M/F
Orientation of Building _____

Natal Number _____
Natal Element_____

Second Resident:
Name _____
Birthdate _____
Sex: M/F
Orientation of Building _____

Natal Number _____
Natal Element_____

ROOMS CHART (Chart 6)

ROOM	LOCATION	PORTENT	SUITABLE FOR
Reception room	......	......	....
Living-room	......	......	....
Dining-room	......	......	....
Kitchen	......	......	....
Bathroom	......	......	....
Bedroom 1	......	......	....
Bedroom 2	......	......	....
Bedroom 3	......	......	....
Bedroom 4	......	......	....
Study	......	......	....
Workshop	......	......	....

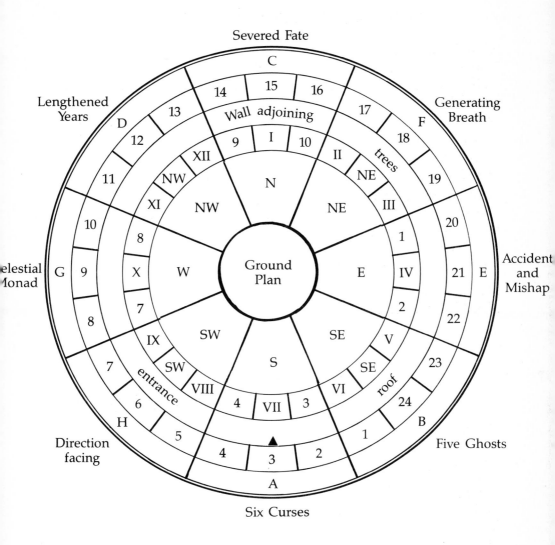

SAMPLE OF COMPLETED LOCATION CHART

Postscript

Today, with a growing awareness of the urgency to cherish the delicate balance of the earth's existence, the art of Feng Shui is coming into greater prominence. It is no longer seen as an ancient mystical Chinese art without relevance to today's needs. Much of the present concern for the earth's delicate and finite resources is in fact a modern manifestation of the original philosophy of Feng Shui. Though the parameters of the practice of Feng Shui may be changing, its moral purpose remains the same after more than two thousand years.

GEOMANTIC SURVEY CHART

Head of household _____

Date of Birth _____

Second principal member of household _____

Date of birth _____

Other members of household _____

_____

_____

_____

_____

_____

Address of premises _____

_____

Orientation _____

GEOMANTIC SURVEY CHART

Head of household _____

Date of Birth _____

Second principal member of household _____

Date of birth _____

Other members of household _____

_____

_____

_____

_____

_____

Address of premises _____

_____

Orientation _____

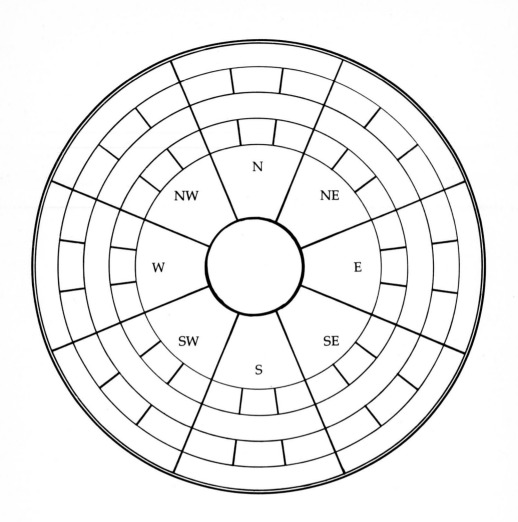

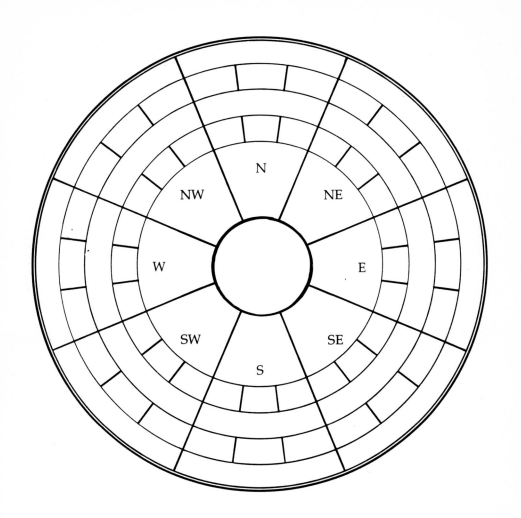

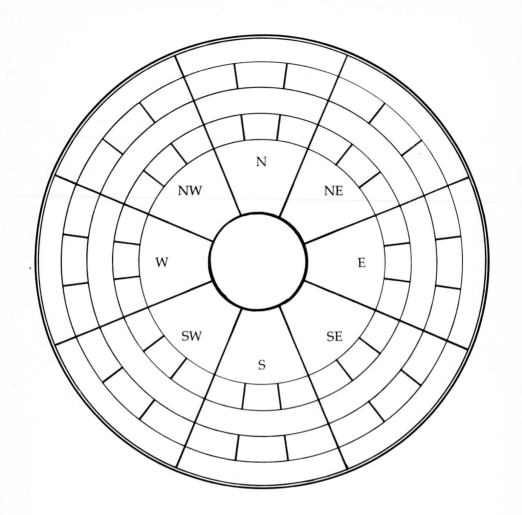

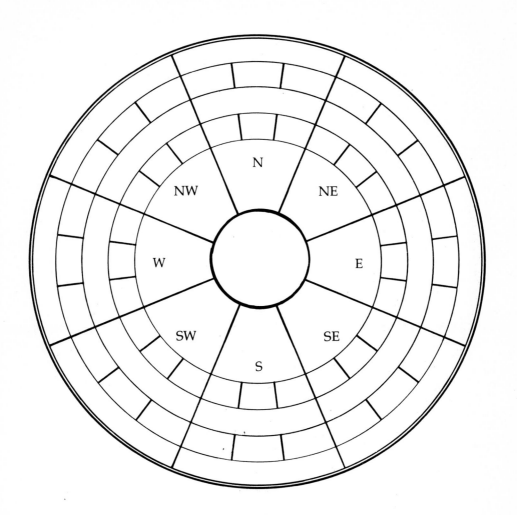

Of further interest . . .

THE CHINESE ASTROLOGY WORKBOOK

How to Calculate and Interpret Chinese Horoscopes

DEREK WALTERS

There is far more to Chinese astrology than the personality types of Rat, Tiger, Monkey, etc. Traditional Chinese astrology is used, in fact, far more for divinatory purposes than for character analysis, and this practical guide therefore follows this bias.

With the aid of a glossary and numerous worksheets and charts, THE CHINESE ASTROLOGY WORKBOOK takes the student into the fascinating world of Chinese astrology: the intricacies of the Chinese calendar; both planetary and Purple Crepe Myrtle astrology (that based on the stars of the Great Bear); the Five Elements, vital to Chinese philosophy as well as their astrology; the Chinese interpretation of the five planets and its fundamental differences from the Western view; constructing and interpreting the final horoscope — all are explained clearly and methodically so that even the complete novice can grasp easily the concepts of Chinese astrology. These include:

- stems and branches
- the Five Elements and planets
- personality profiles
- the rulers of the Purple Palace
- twenty-eight lunar mansions
- imaginary planets

ISBN 0 85030 641 8   £7.99